CHICKEN SOUP FOR THE COFFEE LOVER'S SOUL

CHICKEN SOUP FOR THE COFFEE LOVER'S SOUL

Celebrating the Perfect Blend

Jack Canfield
Mark Victor Hansen
Theresa Peluso

Health Communications, Inc.
Deerfield Beach, Florida
www.hcibooks.com
www.chickensoup.com

We would like to acknowledge the many publishers and individuals who granted us permission to reprint the cited material. Any content not specifically attributed to an author was written by Theresa Peluso. The stories that were penned anonymously, that are in the public domain, or that were written by Jack Canfield, Mark Victor Hansen, or Theresa Peluso are not included in this listing.

Common Grounds. Reprinted by permission of Cynthia Hamond. ©2006 Cynthia Hamond.

Kicking the Habit. Reprinted by permission of Debbie L. Farmer. ©2004 Debbie L. Farmer.

Making Coffee for Dad. Reprinted by permission of Gary Carroll. ©2007 Gary Carroll.

(Continued on page 228)

Library of Congress Cataloging-in-Publication Data

Chicken soup for the coffee lover's soul : celebrating the perfect blend / [compiled by] Jack Canfield, Mark Victor Hansen, Theresa Peluso.
    p. cm.
  ISBN-13: 978-0-7573-0629-7 (trade paper)
  ISBN-10: 0-7573-0629-2 (trade paper)
  1. Coffee.   2. Coffee—Anecdotes.   I. Canfield, Jack, 1944–
II. Hansen, Mark Victor. III. Peluso, Theresa.
TX415.C423 2007
394.1′2—dc22

                                           2007025772

Publisher: Health Communications, Inc.
           3201 S.W. 15th Street
           Deerfield Beach, FL 33442–8190

Cover design by Larissa Hise Henoch
Inside book formatting by Theresa Peluso and Dawn Von Strolley Grove

We dedicate this book to
those who romance the bean
in search of the perfect cup of coffee.

Contents

1. DELECTABLE DELIGHTS

2. TICKLING THE TASTEBUDS

3. RELAXING RENDEZVOUS

Acknowledgments

Compiling, editing, and publishing a book requires the energy and expertise of many people. First, a huge thank-you to our families, who support us with love and encouragement. Thank you Inga, Christopher, Travis, Riley, Oran, Kyle, Patty, Elisabeth, Melanie, and Brian.

Behind the scenes, dozens of talented, enthusiastic staff members, freelancers, and interns keep the wheels turning smoothly at Chicken Soup for the Soul Enterprises, Self-Esteem Seminars, Mark Victor Hansen and Associates, and our publisher, Health Communications, Inc.

The vision and commitment of our publisher, Peter Vegso, brings *Chicken Soup for the Soul* to the world.

Patty Aubery and Russ Kalmaski share this journey with love, laughter, and endless creativity.

Patty Hansen has handled the legal and licensing aspects of each book thoroughly and competently, and Laurie Hartman has been a precious guardian of the Chicken Soup brand.

Michelle Adams, Noelle Champagne, D'ette Corona, Lauren Edelstein, Jody Emme, Teresa Esparza, Jesse Ianniello, Tanya Jones, Debbie Lefever, Barbara LoMonaco, Mary McKay, Dee Dee Romanello, Gina Romanello, Veronica Romero, Brittany Shaw, Shanna Vieyra, Lisa

Williams, and Robin Yerian support Jack's and Mark's businesses with skill and love.

We appreciate the work of HCI's editorial department, directed by Michelle Matriciani, and the HCI creative team, led by Larissa Hise-Henoch, whose efforts make each book special. And thanks to the rest of the staff at HCI, who for their sheer numbers must go nameless, as they get all of our books into readers' hands, copy after copy, with dedication and professionalism.

Readers around the world enjoy *Chicken Soup for the Soul* in more than thirty-six languages because of the efforts of Claude Choquette and Luc Jutras at Montreal Contacts, The Rights Agency.

Our thanks and appreciation go out to the hundreds of writers who shared their stories about their love of coffee. We enjoyed them all and regret that we couldn't publish each and every one of them.

And thank you to the group of coffee lovers who volunteered to help us select these stories: Nora Chesler, Gerald DeShields, Connie Hrbacek, Sharon Mason, Monica Ott, Juanita Pacito, Ellen Packo, Sallie Rodman, Teresa Schleifer, Franklin Shenkman, Lisa Trentacosta, Cathy Ward, Dave Wilkins and Maria Williams.

Introduction

On all but a few occasions, I have started every day of my adult life with a hot cup of coffee—a ritual shared by millions around the world. It takes no effort at all to brew a pot in my modern kitchen with the help of Mister Coffee, but ease and convenience matter little. I've made my morning cup in the dead of winter while camping in the snow, having backpacked for miles into the mountains to leave civilization behind. I didn't even miss a beat when our area took a direct hit from a hurricane. My priorities are clear: a day must begin with a jolt of java.

The history of coffee is full of legend, myth, politics, and drama. Many assume coffee originated in Colombia or Brazil, but it actually has its roots in Ethiopia, where it was discovered before AD 1000. According to legend, the remote highlands were home to a goat herder named Kaldi. One afternoon, his goats failed to return, and after searching for hours he found them at play in a clearing. Kaldi observed that while some frolicked about, others were happily munching on the little red berries from a shiny green shrub. Curious, he tasted a few berries and felt a surge of energy and exhilaration. Anxious to share his newfound discovery, he scooped up some berries, enticed his goats to follow, and headed for the local monastery. At first, the monks decried the berries as a tool of the devil, but soon found themselves captives of the bean.

African nomads crushed the fruit, mixed it with fat, and used it for sustenance on hunting and raiding expeditions. The fermented husks and pulps were even enjoyed as wine. The Arabians brought the plant to the European continent, farmed it, and created a coffee trade, but the Turks were the first to actually make a drink out of the beans in 1453. The beverage became so popular that Turkish law made it legal for a wife to divorce her husband if he did not supply her with enough coffee to last her the day. When Pope Vincent III tasted coffee, he concluded that it would be "a pity to let the infidels have exclusive use of it," and gave it his blessing as an acceptable drink for the Christians.

Coffee was introduced to the United States in the mid-1600s. Over one hundred years later, when the Boston Tea Party cast tea in an unfavorable light, coffee saw a rise in popularity. Within fifteen years, one pound of coffee in New York was worth as much as four acres of land.

By the late 1800s, coffee roasters and mills were commonplace in most cities. When Hills Brothers began packaging coffee in vacuum tins, the small roasters all but disappeared, leaving a few large companies, with names that we recognize today, to carry on. In 1901, a Japanese-American chemist in Chicago created instant coffee, and just a few years after that, a German coffee importer came up with Sanka, the first decaffeinated coffee, after trying to turn a batch of ruined beans into something useful.

When the United States government banned alcohol

during prohibition in the 1920s, coffee sales skyrocketed. Another twenty years, and the U.S. was importing 70 percent of the world's coffee crop for its domestic consumption. American GIs fought World War II with Maxwell House in their K-rations, while hoarding on the home front was common.

Today, coffee is an intricately-woven thread in the tapestry of our lives. We have taken the brewing and blending to a level far exceeding what Achilles Gaggia could have imagined when he invented the espresso machine in Italy after World War II. The plethora of coffee shops we now enjoy give us easy access to some of the world's finest coffee, while our local gas stations usually have a pot on the burner for a quick stop-'n-go. Our cultural consciousness gave birth to Fairtrade, providing the smallest farmers in the most remote areas of the world the opportunity to benefit fairly from man's dependence on the fruit of this bountiful, deep-red berry. Coffee sells for as little as $3 a pound or as much as $200, allowing every economic strata of society a chance to partake.

The perking of a bubbling percolator, the whoosh of a vacuum-sealed can being opened, and the distinctive scrape of scooping grounds into a filter are sounds embedded, almost at a primordial level, in a coffee lover's soul.

But the more insidious allure of coffee is the aroma. Holding a steaming cup and inhaling the redolence of a vapor of steam conjures up the spirits of traders along ancient spice routes. The aura of its heady, rich perfume coaxes us gently from our dreams at the crack of dawn and tantalizes children with its essence for a dozen years before they can partake of the nectar, then more milk than coffee.

The culmination of our ardor is savoring the flavor. With guarded anticipation, a coffee lover discerns the heaviness or lightness of a new roast. We delight in the sensation of dryness at the back of the mouth, characteristic of a desirable acidity. It is at this time that hints of earth, fruit, nuts, even chocolate, are teased from the sated grind.

We asked our writers to reach for their sustenance—Arabica or Robusta. They sipped thoughtfully as they crafted the stories you are about to enjoy, often inspired by the muse of a lucky cup. In these pages we celebrate accomplishments, commiserate tribulations, ameliorate vestiges of pain, and commemorate milestones . . . weaving that intricate tapestry of life.

Come, sit for a while. Relax, let the "to do" list wait a bit longer, and have a cup of coffee with us.

Theresa Peluso

1

DELECTABLE DELIGHTS

Common Grounds

Life is too short for bad coffee.

Author Unknown

t had been a delightful family reunion at our lake cabin in Longville, Minnesota. My parents had come from their home on Maui to spend the summer reconnecting with four generations. It was a week of boating and campfires and laughter that my mother watched and enjoyed from her wheelchair.

Her great-grandchildren seemed to understand that she was fragile, and they would always slow down whenever they tumbled and jumbled too close to her. They knew that her arms were weakened and she couldn't hold them, so they would lean gently into her lap and press their heads against her chest. They felt her love in her laughter and smiles of approval. At night, after she would be helped into bed, all twenty-two of us would line up at her door for a one-at-a-time goodnight kiss. The last one was always my five-year-old granddaughter, Joy. She would flash her sweet, shy smile and then hug her great-grandmother.

One rainy day, with the men forced in from fishing and the children content to watch a movie instead of tubing and swimming, the women decided to go into town together for a ladies' coffee outing. We preened and dressed and campaigned for my mother to go with us. "No, no," she said with her limited speech ability. But we kept insisting, explaining how easy it would be to get her wheelchair into the coffee shop, that we wouldn't stay longer than she would be comfortable, and that it wouldn't be as fun and definitely not complete without her. We all cheered when she finally nodded yes.

My sister helped her get ready, and my daughters wheeled her to the van. For a few more minutes, the cabin screen door creaked and thudded as last-second "I'll-be-right-backs" were shouted, and forgotten items from lipsticks to diapers were retrieved, followed by the shuffling of car seats and the slamming of car doors until everyone was finally settled. Joy stood quietly by, enjoying all the happy busyness.

"Come on, Joy, jump in my car. You come with Grandma!" I tickled her into a hug, looking forward to being alone with her and her chatter. She climbed into the back seat, buckled in and sat, curly-haired and summer-tanned, with her pink, big-girl purse set primly on her lap.

"Grandma," she said, "I like going to coffee with the ladies."

"Well, you are a young lady now," I assured her.

"When I go to town, I usually go for ice cream," she said as she clicked open her purse and rifled inside until she found her little coin bag. She shook it to take measure of the pennies, nickels, dimes, and quarters she had earned. She was too young to notice that her ice-cream purchases were always supplemented by Grandpa and Grandma, or her aunts and uncles, or Dad's and Mom's dollars.

"How much will my coffee cost?" she asked, concerned. "I did have a lot of monies, but now I only have some monies."

"Sweetie pie, it's my treat. You can have any fruit icee you like. I want to celebrate being with you." She smiled as she dropped her coin bag into her purse. I knew she was both glad to hear the words of love, and happy that she could save her money for another ice-cream trip to town.

"Great-Grandma was really sick once, wasn't she?" Joy asked.

"Yes, Joy. We are very blessed that she is still with us."

"When you were my age, could she used to walk?"

"She sure could. She walked me to school and carried me up the stairs to bed. She ran alongside my bike when my dad took off the training wheels. I remember the kitchen on cold winter mornings, with my mother cooking at the stove and the smell of coffee mixing with the warmth of breakfast. I remember the first time I realized that my mother was beautiful. She walked down the front stoop of our house and sat down to watch us play. She was wearing a pretty flowered sweater and soft coral lipstick, her coffee cup nestled in her hands."

Time wavered for me. I saw myself and my granddaughter's reflections in the rearview mirror, and yet, for those few moments, I had been a child again. I teared up for the tenderness of it.

"That's why you are so happy to bring Great-Grandma to coffee, right Grandma?" Joy said.

"You're right, sweetie. Coffee will always make me think of my mother. I guess I want to take every chance I can get to show her that I love her."

"You want to celebwate her," Joy smiled.

We all entered the Common Grounds coffee shop with a whirl of activity. My mother beamed and clapped when we rolled her wheelchair up the ramp, and the deep whiff of coffee greeted us as we opened the door. We found a large table in the home-style comfort and then went to the counter to choose our coffee flavors and desserts, pay for our orders, and relax with our oversized cups of coffee.

It was while I was waiting for Joy's drink that I noticed her little hand reaching up to the counter. Too short to see the top, she stretched, carefully placing each of her coins, side by side, all eighty-seven cents of it.

"Joy, honey, you can put your money back in your purse and save it for ice cream." I stroked her curly hair. "I am celebrating you, remember?"

"I know, Grandma, but I want to buy Great-Grandma's coffee," she said quietly, with all the wisdom of the young and the shared knowledge of the generations. "I want to celebwate her, too."

Cynthia Hamond

What Is It?

Coffee is a tree, a fruit, and a beverage.

The tree is a small evergreen with clusters of fragrant white flowers that mature into deep-red fruit.

The pit of the deep-red coffee cherry shelters the bean that is the center of every coffee lover's universe.

The outer skin of the cherry is bitter and thick. The fruit beneath the skin is very sweet and similar to a grape. Beneath the fruit is a thin, slippery layer of skin, which protects the blue-tinted translucent beans.

A coffee tree takes five years to mature, and each tree yields approximately a pound of roasted beans annually. Most coffee cherries produce two beans.

Kicking the Habit

Decaffeinated coffee is the devil's blend.

Author Unknown

 haven't wanted to talk to anyone about this, but last week my husband came downstairs for breakfast and caught me yelling at the toaster. Much to his credit, he didn't take sides. Instead, he just patted my shoulder and said, "Honey, I think you need to cut down on your caffeine."

"What do you mean?" I said. "I can handle my coffee. It's not my fault the toaster your mother gave us for Christmas has a temperamental attitude. I pushed down the handle, and it's just sitting there, refusing to heat up. And for your information, buddy, I have better things to do than hang around here all morning waiting for it to feel like making toast. So I ask you, then, what am I supposed to do? What? What? WHAT?" I grabbed him by the lapels.

"Now, maybe it's me," he continued, "but lately, you seem a little, well, edgy."

Believe me, I am as shocked as you are. Like nearly everyone else on the planet, I have about one, maybe two cups of coffee a day—especially if you don't count the cup or two of pre-coffee that I drink in the morning until I can get to my real cup at the coffee bar down the street. And I've always considered my after-dinner cups of instant as more of a nightcap. So I did what any devoted wife would do: I called my friend Barb for a second opinion.

"Say, have I been a little, you know, testy lately?" I asked. There was silence for a moment.

"Well," she said finally, "the other day you did yell at the cart corral at the grocery store for taking up a good parking space."

Okay, so maybe, just maybe, my husband was right. But I've been on this Earth long enough to know I can function just fine without coffee. I'm not some kind of weak addict who is dependent upon a stimulant to get through my day. No-sir-ee. So the next day, just to show him what I was made of, I stopped drinking coffee cold turkey. Now, I know what you're thinking. Doing anything "cold turkey" is a very, very bad idea. And you're right. After all, there's a reason they call it that, and I suspect it's because turkeys, as far as animals go, aren't a very smart bunch. But I wasn't thinking about all this back then. I only knew that it was just as easy to drink decaffeinated herbal tea for breakfast as coffee. Why, after only one cup, I could feel all of the caffeine rushing out of my body and being replaced with healthy, disease-fighting antioxidants.

Now, all of this healthiness and good nutrition would've been great, but there was one particular drawback: by mid-morning, my eyeballs felt as if they were hanging somewhere down around my knees and were being kicked every time I took a step.

"Stop yelling, for gosh sakes!" I snapped at my five-year-old son.

"I didn't say anything, Mom. That was the cat."

But what did I expect? Any fool knows that you can't just go around cutting out prominent substances from your diet without going through some signs of withdrawal. That's probably why, when I called my friend Julie to tell her about my new caffeine-free way of life, all that came out was "jummgfhuppmm."

After that, I drank another cup of tea to try to wake myself up. And another. "Mommy, you don't look so good," my son said as I finished off my seventh cup. In the afternoon, I had a hunch, although I could be wrong, that there was a little man inside my head pounding on an anvil. So I tried reading the newspaper to get my mind off the pain, but I couldn't concentrate on a sentence long enough to make it to the end. Somewhere in the middle, I would start staring into space and think about things like high-speed Internet access or the wondrous miracle of life or where, exactly, do all of the lids to Tupperware go.

Then it occurred to me that perhaps smelling coffee wouldn't hurt. I mean, just one or two little sniffs. But, as I opened the lid on the can, something else occurred to me: if I drank a cup of coffee, I'd still be irritable, overly sensitive, and listless. In fact, I'd feel the VERY SAME way I'm feeling now. But my headache would be gone and, with a little luck, I'd get my mental edge back. So I made a cup. Just a little one. But don't worry, if my husband finds out, I'll tell him that the toaster drove me to it.

Debbie Farmer

Making Coffee for Dad

Nothing will make a father swear before the
children quicker than a cup of poor coffee.

K. Hubbard

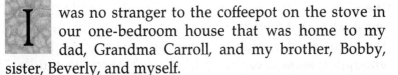

I was no stranger to the coffeepot on the stove in our one-bedroom house that was home to my dad, Grandma Carroll, and my brother, Bobby, sister, Beverly, and myself.

How we dreaded making Dad's coffee when it was our turn. He'd say, "Gary, make me a cup of coffee." I'd be watching Johnny Weissmuller wrestle with the lions or alligators in *Tarzan* on a Sunday afternoon on our black-and-white TV and didn't want to leave the room. Dad liked his coffee black. It wasn't hard to make—just heat the water, add two spoons of instant coffee into a cup of boiling water, and carry it to him.

One day, a mischievous teenage thought came into my mind. The next time he asked me to make him a cup of coffee, I'd fix it so he'd never ask me to make him another one, ever! I didn't have to wait very long to hatch my devious plot; he asked me to make him a cup the next day.

Turning on the stove, I placed the old blue coffeepot on the burner and let the water come to a boil. Chuckling while opening the lid to the instant coffee, and hoping he wouldn't get sick, I added four heaping spoons of coffee into the waiting cup of boiling water. Acting like nothing was different, and walking the few steps from the kitchen to Dad's homemade desk, I was certain this would be the last time I'd be making coffee for my dad. He thanked me as I set the cup on his desk and walked away.

Surreptitiously glancing in his direction from my post in the living room, I was amazed. Dad was actually drinking the coffee. He even finished it! No way! "Gary Lee! Come here!" my dad's voice boomed, just as I anticipated. *What extra chores is he going to assign me this time?* I wondered.

Walking over to him, with my head slouched down like a puppy that's been bad, but laughing in my heart, I slowly made my way over to the warden to get the bad news. Raising my head, I looked into his piercing, sky-blue eyes and . . . his broad smile. My dad opened his mouth and said, "Gary, this is the best cup of coffee I've ever had in my life!" Well, I knew my days of making coffee for Dad were far from over. In fact, as you would expect, my turn came more often than it did before I executed my brilliant plan.

One day, the tables were turned. My stomach was hurting so bad and the pain would not stop, so Dad, being the expert at homemade remedies, made me a cup of coffee. Only this coffee was different. He added a teaspoon of coffee, some salt, pepper, Tabasco sauce, spices, lemon juice, and other ingredients into the cup of hot water. After being made to drink all of it, I heaved up the contents of my stomach and was soon better. I never again let Dad know if, or when, my stomach was hurting.

No doubt, that experience is part of the reason why I have never acquired a taste for coffee. But I did acquire a taste for plenty of other things from my dad before he passed on; kindness, a love of God, the value of service, how to be a good man—and, of course, how to make one really good cup of coffee.

Gary Carroll

Café Martín

I judge a restaurant by the bread
and by the coffee.

Burt Lancaster

 -o-f-f-e. . . .
The word eliminated me from the spelling bee and humiliated my mother to think I couldn't spell the name of my family's favorite beverage.

I hadn't wanted to be in the spelling bee in the first place. My mother insisted. The only thing she enjoyed as much as her morning coffee was bragging, and there'd been a long, dry spell. Obviously desperate, she convinced herself I could win the spelling bee hands down. When I came home from school each afternoon, she'd drill me on spelling words. Coffee wasn't among them.

As the school principal confidently spelled coffee correctly, I looked down from the stage and recognized the fabric from the new dress my mother had been making. She sat in the second row, mouth agape, face red with shame. I wondered if I'd be cutting a switch after school that day.

No matter how it's spelled, coffee became the barometer of my soul, my moods, my health, and my social life. When

I don't crave a cup of steaming java, it doesn't take a doctor to tell me I'm sick. Some of my most cherished memories are made up of events involving friends, relatives, good times, and a pot of coffee on the stove. My husband and I visited different coffee houses every weekend, and eventually we chose favorites.

There was never any doubt that Café Martin was head and shoulders above the others. It was a *Cheers* knockoff, a place where everybody knew your name. Martin was a newly transported Londoner who not only served the best coffee in town, but some of the best food as well. Scotch eggs, English breakfasts, sausage rolls, his own brand of spicy curry, and countless other dishes were made in the back kitchen.

And there were groceries, too. Specialty items were imported from England. If you spoke without a British accent at Café Martin, you were clearly in the minority.

Martin was a swarthy, muscular man, his coal-black hair giving way to a little gray. He was several inches shy of six feet, and I never saw him wear anything but shorts and a Hawaiian shirt, English jersey or a West Ham shirt, the latter promoting his beloved soccer. Martin loved babies, too. He didn't care if they were smiling or crying; he opened his arms to them and carried them around on his shoulder. He introduced them to the joys of whipped cream, filling small dishes for them as a special treat.

By late morning, you'd usually find Martin sitting outside at one of the tables in front of the café. He'd have a cigarette in one hand and a cup of coffee in the other. He held court. There was no other way to describe it. Someone even brought him a director's chair. Bright and quick-witted, I don't think anyone ever got the best of him. Customers joked that we always got abuse along with our coffee, but he was a kind man. One customer was depressed over a divorce, and Martin tried to find help for him. A death in the family, and he'd be on your doorstep with your favorite dish. If someone hit on hard times, Martin never hesitated to dip into the till. He wasn't rich, but money changed hands often. He was that kind of man.

Martin was a special brew of coffee, one of a kind, a kind we all loved, a kind who ignored the chest pains that signaled the heart attack that killed him. "Only indigestion," he'd assured his wife.

The local cop on the beat was a customer and Martin's best friend. He spoke through tears at Martin's memorial service and shared some of their escapades. One in particular delighted him. His squad car became a favorite topic of conversation at Café Martin's after it was involved in several minor smash-ups. Concentrating on the cholesterol-lowering oatmeal that had become his afternoon snack, he didn't notice Martin leaving the café, but when he finished his oatmeal and returned to his squad car, customers' faces were pressed to the window of Café Martin's. The squad car shimmered in the Florida sunlight. Always the helpful friend, Martin had covered it in bubble wrap.

We continue to miss Martin, especially the abuse. But every cup of coffee is a reminder of a wonderful memory. And Martin taught me how to spell coffee with only one "e." L-O-V-E.

Ruth Coe Chambers

Mediterranean Coffee

Coffee has two virtues:
it is wet, and it is warm.

Dutch Proverb

t annoys me when so-called "experts" write endless words on the world's best coffee. Although I
live in Scotland, my grandmother was German,
and so I was brought up on coffee. My grandparents had
a favorite coffee. So did my mum, but they didn't claim it
as the best ever. Pillar Desabio did, but then on reflection,
I have to concede there were exceptions in her case!

When I first met Pillar, she was about seven years old,
and I was on my first visit to my cousin's house on the
Spanish island of Majorca. Pillar Desabio lived next door
to my aunt and uncle, and she was my cousin Jackie's best
friend. Pillar's mum and dad ran a small tourist hotel on
the island, and my aunt often had Pillar to stay at her
house. She was such a good-natured and contented girl,
and although she was brought up on Spanish food, she
was always eager to try anything British that my aunt
made.

The only thing that Pillar would never touch was my
aunt's coffee. My aunt just assumed Pillar didn't like it

until her mum told my aunt that coffee was one of Pillar's favorite drinks. She tried persuading her, but could only ever get her to drink soft drinks. Finally, when Jackie and her folks came to visit us in Scotland, they brought Pillar with them. By this time, the girls were both around thirteen years old and more outspoken. Jackie complained about most things, but then that was her way. The only thing Pillar complained about was the British coffee. She had tried it at the London airport, in our house, and in one or two other places, and it was so bad to her taste that she could never finish one cup. She was amazed that we could drink such stuff that tasted nothing like real coffee.

A year later, we went to visit them all in Majorca again, and this time Pillar's parents invited us to the hotel for a meal. Jackie and I went along early to meet up with Pillar and found her in the hotel kitchen. All along the front of the bay were little hotels like her parents', plus cafés and bars. She sat us down at the hotel's kitchen table and told us, "Now I will let you taste real coffee!" She came over with a metal coffeepot and poured out a cup of quite strong-looking, black coffee. Having already tried Spanish espresso coffee, I didn't mind. I quite liked the very strong kind. I took one sip, and my eyes met Jackie's, who was all too aware of what I would think of my first taste of this "special brew." I could have choked her for not warning me as I tried to swallow and smile, and look suitably impressed at the same time. Not easy when it tasted more like black sea water than coffee!

In those days, Spain was not part of the European Common Market, and so rules on water supplies and things were much "looser." Somewhere along the line to this hotel and others in the area, seawater was being mixed with drinking water! This "real" coffee was quite salty, but I forced myself to drink it as Pillar was standing there watching me, and I didn't want to hurt her feelings.

"Isn't that the best coffee you have ever tasted?" she enthused.

"Pillar, I have never tasted any coffee like this before!" I managed to say to her satisfaction.

Now, when I hear the experts claim this one or that as the best in the world, I smile to myself and think of Pillar. She sat down beside us that day and sipped at a large mug of her mum's coffee, and her face glowed with pride, firmly convinced that no one could make it like this.

"They say the best coffee is from Brazil," she told me, "but they do not make it like we do in the Mediterranean." To think that is because they were making it from the Mediterranean itself!

Joyce Stark

Ways to Brew the Bean:
Ibrik (or Cezves or Briki)

The ibrik is a long-handled, Turkish coffeepot that produces one of the most exotic forms of brewed coffee. Originally made from brass or hammered copper, it was designed to brew coffee in the hot desert sand, but today's stainless-steel models are well adapted to the stove. An ibrik's pot is generally small and always narrower at the top than the bottom—a shape essential in brewing a proper Turkish coffee.

To make it, add water until the ibrik is two-thirds full, then add sugar if desired. Use a very fine, almost powdered grind of a Turkish blend coffee. For every three ounces of water, use one heaping teaspoon of coffee.

The coffee forms a cap over the water, and as you heat the ibrik, the boiling water bubbles up through the coffee grounds. When the water foams up, remove the ibrik from the burner (or the hot Sahara desert sand), and once it has settled, bring it back to the heat source.

Once your coffee has foamed up three times, it is done. If the coffee boils in the ibrik, it means there is not enough coffee. For larger ibriks, experiment with your quantity. Stir and serve in espresso cups. Let the grounds settle before drinking.

Coffee with Milk, please

Coffee in England is just toasted milk.

Christopher Fry

ver the years, coffee has become my test of a good restaurant—not just the taste, but the way it is served. I'll order coffee, then pause and add very firmly, "with a lot of milk, please." If the server gets it right, the restaurant passes, and I'll go back. If not, I might give the restaurant a second chance, but if it fails a second time, I'll look for another place to eat. I've spent a lot of time looking.

At eighteen, I found the perfect formula for coffee—one that I've never changed. Long before most North Americans discovered the joys of café latte, I drank my coffee two-thirds coffee, one-third milk. Too little milk meant a strong, bitter brew. Too much, and the coffee had no taste. The correct amount of milk smoothed out the rough edges of the coffee and cooled it to the perfect temperature. I loved the warmth as the liquid filled my mouth and trickled down my throat.

At home, my coffee-drinking habits were accepted, or at least tolerated. My mother would smile and ask, "Want a little coffee to go with your milk?" I'd nod and watch as she carefully poured my coffee, leaving lots of room in the cup for milk. My older sister looked at me with disdain, but older sisters often do that. My father, who drank his coffee so hot it would have scalded most people, just shook his head. I didn't care. I had found what worked for me.

Restaurants proved more difficult. Whether the restaurant was a greasy spoon that used individual single-serving plastic containers of milk or cream, or an elegant upscale establishment that used silver jugs, it didn't matter. At each restaurant, I went through the same routine. Most of the time, the wait staff brought cream instead of milk or had to be reminded to bring additional milk with each refill. The first time one of my friends heard me order, she asked, "Why do you emphasize the milk, not the coffee?" A coffee aficionado, she thought paying more attention to the milk than the coffee was criminal.

Over the next couple of months, my friend and I developed a Sunday ritual that involved a big breakfast with three cups of coffee, followed by a walk to work off some of the calories. We tried out different restaurants in the area until we finally settled on one restaurant, partly because of the food, but mostly because of the service. The first time we

An Olfactory Primer

Bitterness, acidity, and astringency are potent characteristics often attributed to coffee. These are sensed orally when certain compounds in the coffee interact with the papillae (little hairs) on the tongue.

Aroma is sensed nasally by smelling the coffee, or retro-nasally when the coffee has been swallowed, and the volatile aromatic compounds drift back into the nasal passage.

went there, I did the usual "with lots of milk, please." The waitress brought six little containers. I beamed. When I asked for a refill, she gave me six more containers. I beamed some more. Then six more for my third cup of coffee. I outbeamed the sun. My friend sighed in relief because we were running out of restaurants to try.

The second time we went there, we sat in the same section. The waitress smiled when she saw us and brought a plate filled with twenty individual milk containers. For the next forty-five minutes, she kept the coffee coming—hot and strong. My friend liked the coffee; I liked the service. The waitress got a nice tip.

After going there for about five months, we arrived at the restaurant later than usual one morning. Our regular waitress's section was filled. We nodded to her as we chose a table further back. A different waiter took our order. As he went to the coffee station, I noticed our waitress speak to him and point in our direction. Sure enough, a moment later we had fresh cups of coffee, complete with a plate filled with a mountain of plastic milk containers. I relaxed. I had truly found a restaurant and staff who understood that good service, as well as coffee, comes in many forms. For me, it comes with milk, please.

Harriet Cooper

In the Meantime

Actually, this seems to be the basic need of the human heart in nearly every great crisis—a good, hot cup of coffee.

Alexander King

I have two cups of coffee a week. For sure. One on Monday morning. And another on Thursday morning. And I really look forward to them.

For several years now, I have gotten up at the crack of dawn, like I used to when I was teaching, and have barreled down Arrow Boulevard in the direction of St. Catherine's. Mass is at eight, so I make sure I get there before the church bells ring.

After Mass, my friend Jo and I head to her house for breakfast. As soon as our feet hit the kitchen floor, Jo twists the knob on her gas range, and the iridescent flame begins its dance under the kettle of water that has been waiting for our return. She then adds fresh coffee granules to the bottom of a European-style, glass coffeepot, pours the boiling water in it, and sets it on the table. I wait a few minutes and then push down the little black knob in the center of its lid, sending the finished product rising to the top of the pot. And, voilà, the coffee is ready to be poured into the white porcelain cups sitting in their matching saucers. I grab for the milk; Jo takes just sugar.

There's something comforting about having a cup of coffee with a friend. It just tastes better. As Jo and I sip our coffee, accompanied by hot-buttered toast with apricot jam, we talk about everything. But somehow, sharing the kitchen table, she on one side and I on the other, it's easy to open our hearts and express our innermost feelings.

"I miss my mom," I whisper. "She lived for ninety-three years before that brazen thief tiptoed into her life and shamelessly stole her from us. It was bad enough that he took her memory, her mind. Why did he have to take her, too?" And I begin to cry, my tears falling freely. The pain is still fresh.

My friend listens, sipping her coffee. Tears fill her eyes, too. And the healing begins.

She was a good mother. I don't remember a Sunday dinner when there wasn't homemade pasta on the table in a bowl big enough to feed an army. Everything was home-made—the sauce, the bread, even the sausage. And for dessert, a cup of hot coffee and homemade apple pie. The aroma of freshly brewed coffee always filled the kitchen.

Dad liked his coffee strong, espresso-style. "Like in the old country," he would say. Mom liked her coffee with cream and sugar, the shade of coffee-colored stockings. And I liked mine with milk. A café latte sometimes. A cappuccino, other times. We'd all sit and talk for hours— my mom, dad, sisters, brother and I—our coffee cups clinking in rhythm like a synchronized symphony.

"Remember, Mom, when we couldn't find Grandpa at the train station and . . ."

". . . and he was already on the train," Mom chimes in, laughing. "He loved to travel. He was always the first one on board."

Mom used to remember everything. If you wanted to know anything about anything, just ask Mom. And then one day, she couldn't remember where the bathroom was. Or if she had breakfast. Or that we were there with her when we stepped out of the room for a moment. In the end, she couldn't even remember how many children and grandchildren she had, let alone their names.

And so it became my turn to make the coffee. I would fill her big brown mug with the word "Mom" etched on it in bold, curvy letters, and then get myself the one with the brightly colored Christmas tree painted on it. No matter what time of the year, I loved the feeling of Christmas in my hands. It seemed to offer so much promise.

Sipping our coffee in our favorite mugs, we welcomed that time together. Sometimes we talked; sometimes we didn't. Occasionally, Mom would say something, and a few minutes later she would say it again. And then, again. I would hold my promise cup a little tighter in my hands. I knew that Alzheimer's bandit was taking her away from us. And there was nothing we could do to stop it.

These are some of the thoughts I carry with me to the Monday and Thursday morning table when I share the flavor of coffee and words with a good friend. Our white porcelain cups sit in their matching saucers, taking in our conversation. And, suddenly, everything feels right with the world. When I leave, I take that warm, cozy feeling with me, tucking it away into my heart until the next time we meet.

In the meantime, there are mornings when I sit at my own kitchen table, sipping my coffee from the big brown mug with the word "Mom" etched on it in bold, curvy letters. I welcome its comfort and the memories of my mother like she used to be—well, vibrant, alive. And I hold my cup a little tighter, the aroma of fresh coffee and beautiful memories filling the room.

Lola Di Giulio De Maci

Ways to Brew the Bean: French Press (or Bodum)

A delicious cup of coffee, and one of the easiest you will ever make, can be made with the French press.

The press consists of a glass carafe, which comes in many sizes, and a wire mesh screen attached to a plunger.

To make coffee in a French press, bring water almost to a boil in a kettle. One key is to pre-warm the carafe just before adding your coffee as you would "hot the pot" when making tea.

Add a medium coarse to coarse grind of coffee to the pre-warmed, empty carafe in the same proportions you would for your favorite drip coffee.

Pour your nearly boiled water into the carafe, wait 2–3 minutes for the coffee to settle, and then press the plunger down to filter the coffee. Your coffee is ready to serve.

Using a French press ensures that no oils are trapped by a filter and the water is never too hot, although there may be a bit of sediment in your cup.

caffeine and a Smile

Once you wake up and smell the coffee,
it's hard to go back to sleep.

Fran Drescher

he alarm jolted me into the dark predawn. Still sleepy, I slogged through my morning routine— shower, dress, dry hair, apply makeup, pat the cat, feed the fish, pack food and drink, pat the cat, pack workout clothes, kiss husband, son, and cat good-bye.

I stepped into the frigid air to find my truck glazed with ice. I started the engine, put heat and blower on high, and headed for work when the ice had melted enough for me to see through the windshield. I shivered and looked forward to hot coffee. Every morning I stop for coffee to drink on the way to work. I'm a tea drinker the rest of the day, but my morning coffee was a habit I wouldn't give up. I welcomed the sharp taste that coaxed my eyes open, and the caffeine that melted the sludge in my veins and got it flowing again.

This morning, the line for coffee was long; others were also waiting for their warm eye-opener on a winter morning. I snailed around to the speaker and placed my order. "May I help you?" came the staticky voice. "Yes, a medium

French vanilla with skim milk. No sugar, please." "Drive up, please." But the line didn't move. There were three cars idling in front of me, sending spumes of exhaust drifting into the frosty air.

I sat as minutes ticked by. Sixty seconds became five minutes and grew to seven. I would definitely be late to work. Not a harmless few minutes, but a serious-chunk-of-time late. Irritation set in. It's one thing to be a little late due to my own choices—patting the cat, stopping for coffee—but now somebody else was making me late, and I was annoyed. Rolling down my window, I stuck my head out to see what the holdup was. My frustration formed a steamy cloud when my breath hit the chill.

A young woman in the first car was fluffing her hair and applying lipstick. What had she ordered that took ten minutes to prepare? She appeared to have all the time in the world. She checked her teeth in her rearview mirror, then more hair fluffing. I began to dislike her. Thoughtless and vain, she was making me late. After thirteen minutes, the cashier handed fluff woman a bulging bag, then another, then a third and a fourth. Fluffy handed the cashier some money, change was made, and she was off in a cloud of exhaust, probably on time for work. I was later than ever, and anxiety kicked at my stomach.

When I pulled up to get my one little coffee, I grumbled to the cashier about rude, selfish people as I paid. I stuck my coffee in the cup holder and pulled into traffic. The car filled with that roasted bean tang, acrid but delightful, the same tang that woke me as a child. Its bittersweet fragrance teased and promised that the first mouth-warming sip would jump-start my morning. I knew just how far I needed to drive to let it cool enough not to scald my throat. When I peeled back the plastic tab for a sip, I noticed a symbol on the cup's lid. A small smiley face drawn in black Sharpie marker beamed at me. Despite my anxiety at being late and my frustration at fluff woman, I smiled to myself—just a little.

I took a sip, warm and strong, and smiled again at the unknown worker who'd drawn the familiar symbol of good will. Another sip, another smile. I pulled into the parking lot at work well over fifteen minutes late, but I had an excuse should I need one: A nice woman at the coffee shop was buying coffee for her office workmates. She held up the line a bit.

My boss didn't see me as I hurried past his office. I smiled. Later in the morning, as I microwaved the last of the coffee in my cup, I felt again the power of a simple smile, stronger than any jolt of caffeine. I thought of the woman who had delayed me. I wondered if her cup had a smile, too. I hoped so.

Ruth Douillette

A Way of Life

I have measured out my life
with coffee spoons.

T. S. Eliot

he addiction, if it can be called such, began as a small seed during my childhood. My mother allowed me a very small cup of coffee, watered down, of course, with plenty of sugar. It was a rare treat, and only offered on special occasions, like when company was staying over after dinner, or my dad was playing his guitar in the evenings. Even though I recall the sweetness of the coffee, I recall even more the meaning behind the coffee treat: it always accompanied some very special event.

As the years passed, I married, had children, and moved away from home. During those ten years away, I rarely drank coffee. Too busy getting my PHT (Putting Hubby Through college) degree and raising kids, I never felt the occasion for coffee. Just drinking it on the fly was not my idea of coffee. Coffee was both a noun, an adjective ("I feel like coffee this morning"), an event ("let's do coffee"), and a way of life that I wasn't ready for yet.

After four years in the military, four years of college, and two years working, our little family decided to move back to our home state of Idaho. Each state we had lived in had produced a son for us: Illinois/Jason, South Dakota/Jeremy, and Oregon/Joel. When I left Idaho at sixteen years old, I swore I would never return to the small "hick" town. But having kids changes a person's perspective, and here I was, three small boys in tow, coming back to raise them on the same property where I was raised—ten acres of pasture and woodland near Moscow Mountain, north Idaho. By now, the place held a powerful allure that I couldn't resist. I was homesick for the land, and I wanted my sons to know it like I had.

My husband built up a small business on the property, and we set about creating a country life for ourselves. While the boys and I tilled the soil and planted vegetables, my husband built handcrafted kitchen cabinets and furniture in the little shop we had remodeled. Both sets of grandparents still lived there, and having us home enriched their lives. Since we moved away shortly after we married, I never really got to know my in-laws. I knew a few things about my mother-in-law: she hated to cook, she loved to knit, and she walked over to the local coffee shop each morning to mingle with girlfriends.

After school started that fall and the boys were gone all day, I drove into town to see what the coffee-shop attraction was about. This was before the popularity of lattes and mochas, so specialty coffees had nothing to do with the gathering, and neither did the quality of the drip coffee. Yet it was around the coffee that the group poured out their hearts and souls to one another. It was here, over the steam and aroma of bottomless coffee cups, where I got to know my mother-in-law, where we cried together over the loss of a pastor's wife, where I shared I was pregnant again and began to drink decaf—which had no effect on the quality of the meetings.

After my fourth son, Jesse, was born, my coffee-shop friends were the first to meet him. When he was two years old, I brought him with me to coffee, and sometimes he would sit with the old farmers and play cards. On his fourth birthday, the waitress baked him a birthday cake. By now, my mother-in-law, Virginia, had become my best friend.

After Jesse started kindergarten, things began to unravel at home. My mother-in-law sensed the change, but was discreet, only saying that she'd missed me at the coffee shop again. A year later, the boys and I left, and a few years later, my mother-in-law passed away. For years, I didn't drink coffee. I felt that I had no occasion, and on some level that I didn't deserve the experience. Not only that, it conjured up memories of good times past and the best years of my life, which had been cut short far too soon.

As I began to put my life back together and meet new friends, I started seeing small coffee stands on the corners of the street. "Have you tried a latte?" a girlfriend asked. "What's a latte?" I asked, picturing something too milky and sweet. I was used to the strong, black stuff. Nonetheless, I agreed to try one, and before long, double Irish cream lattes became a part of my life. But this time, it was different. While before, coffee meant friends and conversation, now it meant a peaceful morning over a book, a new era of my life that was grounded in whom I had become.

One morning, my youngest son, now grown, came by the house with a triple mint mocha in hand. He sat on the couch and shared with me that he was getting married. On another morning, similar coffee in hand, I learned that he was having a son. My three older boys have grown and moved away to other towns, but when they come home to visit, I whisk them off to the nearest coffee shop to catch up.

On some Saturday mornings, Jesse will call and say, "Hey, wanna go get a coffee? April and Kaden are still sleeping." And I know that's not what he really means. What he really means is, I want to spend time with you. I want to talk about something meaningful. I want to connect with you over this drink—this thing called coffee that really means so much more than that.

Coffee has been a catalyst in my life, and part of so many important, noteworthy events that I can't consider it just a drink. Over coffee, I recently found that my mother has lung cancer; my nephew's wife is having twins; my youngest son and wife are expecting their second child. Coffee, whether good or bad, has a way of creating relationships.

Cheryl Dudley

"I'm down to one cup of coffee a day."

Revelations of a Good Coffee Fanatic

As soon as coffee is in your stomach,
there is a general commotion.
Ideas begin to move ... similes arise,
the paper is covered. Coffee is your ally,
and writing ceases to be a struggle.

Honoré de Balzac

I'd been working for a community newspaper in 2005 and was searching for story ideas when I noticed a new coffee house in the neighborhood. Where had that bright yellow "coffee" sign come from? Last time I'd noticed, the building had been an abandoned frame shop. Now it was Panther City Coffee Company. I went in with my mother one evening after work and came out with a great story of this locally owned, family business. A whole new universe had opened up before me.

In my experience, coffee came in three forms: whole bean, ground, and brewed—usually in a bag or can from the grocery store, in whatever brand was cheapest. If I was feeling particularly financially flush, or there was a great sale, I occasionally bought bulk coffee from Starbucks or another similar retailer. Coffee came from Juan Valdez and his decrepit donkey. Right? I didn't think about it any further than that. I didn't have a clue about what it went through to get to me, or how old the coffee was when it did get to me. Coffee was coffee was coffee. Right? Wrong. Way wrong. Very, very wrong. Juan Valdez fooled me!

What I discovered in the Panther City Coffee Company is a coffee house known to roast their own beans on-site. That explained the unusual smell, not as heady as a bakery, that had permeated the neighborhood since the shop opened. Until I interviewed the general manager and resident roaster, I had no idea that coffee beans went stale after only two measly weeks, or that once ground, coffee goes stale in about twenty minutes. I was stunned. I was floored. I had no idea. I'd had longer relationships with bags and varieties of coffee than I had with some men in my life. And, frankly, until this point, I hadn't cared.

After only a few short visits to my neighborhood java oasis, I now knew there was difference between good coffee and everything else. There is more to coffee than "bold" and "mild" coffee-of-the-day. Really, there is! My geographical knowledge has also grown as I discovered better coffee. I now know that Sulawesi, Mogiana, Tanzanian Peaberry, and Harar not only come from different parts of the world, but are different varieties of coffee bean with different roasting processes for different flavors. Columbia Supremo is dark, while Mexican Altura is mild, and Brazilian Mogiana (a personal favorite) fools you by being a darker roasted, mild coffee. I was thrilled to watch the roasting process while given a history lesson in how coffee was discovered by dancing goats in Ethiopia. Yes, that's right, dancing goats. My world opened up.

I found it difficult to go back to drinking coffee where I couldn't see the roasting date actually on the bag, let alone what hotels try to pawn off on unsuspecting travelers as coffee in those pre-packaged, hotel-room brewers. I always knew that I shouldn't be able to see through the coffee to the bottom of the cup, but now the very thought of consuming such a brew gives me the screaming willies.

Now, there is no turning back. The grocery-store coffee aisle is anathema to me unless it's for filters or other non-coffee products. I no longer look to Starbucks for my morning jolt unless there is no other option. I have discovered honest-to-goodness, fresh-roasted, fresh-brewed coffee. I have been spoiled by the riches provided by this coffee-shop salvation, and I share my newfound awareness with others. In the course of the months that I have been made aware of my coffee shortcomings, I have discovered that I am not alone in the darkness. Others have joined the revolution and the revelation, and we agree on one thing: none of us knew what we were missing until Panther City Coffee Company came along.

I've survived two out-of-town convention trips on hotel coffee-like substances, and have dragged myself into other coffee shops in desperation, when there is no other option. The withdrawal from good coffee is just too painful to contemplate on a regular basis, so now I travel with my own stash. I have taken up the cause—the grinder and the bulk beans I know were roasted within the past fourteen days—and I am going forth.

Good coffee should not be a shock and surprise to discover, but it is a joy to behold once it has been. And I, for one, am a much happier person for having been so enlightened. The lure of the best coffee in the metropolitan area has driven others to go above and beyond the call of duty. To keep our coffee supply coming, patrons of this old-fashioned, please-stay-around, too-Bohemian-for-some-people coffee house have voluntarily washed dishes, done guerrilla marketing, and even donated money to replace what was lost in a break-in. It's all because of the superior product. Good coffee calls to good people. And that, I think, may be the greatest revelation of all.

Rhonda Eudaly

At Its Best

Unprocessed green coffee beans have a long shelf life and can remain in warehouses for months, sometimes years. This is not the case for roasted and ground coffee.

If possible, buy beans directly from a roaster. In general, a roasted bean is at its best within 2–4 days of roasting. Coffee is considered "fresh" for no more than two weeks, so ideally you want to buy only what you will use in a week. Buy the highest quality whole bean and grind it as needed.

Because the coffee bean is porous, experts advise against storing coffee in the refrigerator. Changes in temperature create moisture, and moisture is the enemy. The freezer is acceptable storage for bulk supplies of coffee, but once you remove beans from the freezer, use them. Divide the bulk supply of beans into weekly portions, and wrap those in plastic wrap and freezer bags before packing them into the deep freeze. Remove the weekly portions as you need them. Store the whole beans in a sealed container in a dry, dark place. Glass or ceramic is preferable as it will not affect the essential oils of the beans. Grind just enough beans for the pot you're brewing and match your grind size to your brewing method.

Filtered water is preferred for brewing good coffee, but don't confuse that with distilled water. Filtering improves the taste and odor of water and removes some contaminants by using carbon filters. Distilled water is virtually pure, but the process of distillation adds oxygen molecules that degrade the flavor of coffee. Research has shown that coffee brewed with tap water is actually less bitter than coffee brewed with distilled water.

A Cup of Love

No one can understand the truth until he
drinks of coffee's frothy goodness.

Sheik Abd-al-Kadir

 ot and steaming. That scent, fresh in the morning
air as you rise from bed. Can a smell really be so
darkly rich, so exciting and exotic, so invigorating? I consider certain foods and drinks essential—not to
my health, but to my happiness. Number one on that list
is coffee.

Coffee, in all its many flavors and styles, is everywhere.
My personal favorite is to brew it with a touch of cinnamon, vanilla or cocoa powder in the grounds. Most days,
I'll simply top it off with skim milk and sugar. At night, if
I'm in the mood for something sweeter, I'll add a dollop of
whipped cream.

And sometimes I like it just the way I drank it as a young
boy at my grandfather's knee. Back then, when I was just
eight or nine, my grandfather would start each morning by
brewing a pot of thick, black coffee, so rich and bitter it was
almost espresso. He even made it in an old-fashioned percolator, a four-cup, metal pot that was all hard angles and
sections. A tiny glass bulb at the top allowed a fascinated

boy to watch the liquid bubble up as it brewed.

My grandmother would be bustling around the kitchen, fixing breakfast, setting the table, buttering toast. My parents would be reading the morning paper as golden sunshine lit up the yellow wallpaper of the kitchen.

Once it was ready, Grandfather would pour a half-cup for me, and generously dilute it with sugar and milk. For himself, a touch of milk was all he took.

"Dad, don't give him that. It'll stunt his growth," my mother would always complain.

"Bah! You drank it as a girl. And look at you, tallest one in the family. It's good for you," he'd tell me, passing the steaming cup my way.

Years later, coffee became the cup or two I bought at the local diner or Pancake House on the way to high school. My love of java only grew during college and graduate school. It always amazed me that one beverage could take on so many roles—dessert, morning pick-me-up, study aid, even an excuse to ask someone for a date.

Luckily, I'm not alone among my friends and family in my adoration of the dark nectar. To this day, it's common for several of us to gather at one house or another to enjoy some good conversation over a pot of fresh coffee.

As the years went by, modern technology brought us the Mister Coffee, and then exotic coffee makers by too many companies to name. After them came the home espresso and cappuccino makers. For a while, we'd try to outdo each other by buying the latest coffee-making gadgets, constantly experimenting to create the ultimate, best cup of coffee. We'd grind our own beans, dabble in flavorings, and even keep a variety of sugars in the house, from plain white to my personal favorite, the brown, granulated raw sugar.

And then something interesting happened.

We were at a friend's house one evening, sitting in the kitchen, and she asked us if we wanted coffee.

Of course, the answer was yes.

"I'll put on a fresh pot. I just got a new percolator. It makes the best coffee."

"Percolator?" I hadn't heard that word in over twenty years.

Sure enough, she went to the cabinet and pulled down an old-fashioned coffeepot, almost identical to the one that used to sit on my grandparents' stove. The hour-glass shape, the tiny glass bulb at the top, the soft bubbling sound as the water went up and down.

All the same.

Memories came rushing back in a wave. For a moment, I found myself sitting in a different kitchen, surrounded by family long since gone.

"My grandfather used to have one just like this."

The words interrupted my reverie, and brought me back to the present.

"Mine, too," I said, breathing deeply and filling my nose with the scent of nostalgia.

"Skim milk, one sugar?" my friend asked, placing an oversized coffee mug on the table. We all know how each person takes it.

I smiled. "I think I'll splurge tonight. Whole milk and extra sugar." Grandfather would be proud.

Greg Faherty

Ways to Brew the Bean: Percolator

Percolated coffee has a distinctive quality that has remained popular with campers and outdoorsmen. A medium coarse to coarse grind of coffee is recommended for this type of brewing method.

Most coffee drinkers agree that coffee should never be boiled since high heat tends to result in a bitter flavor. However, boiling is part of the percolator process. Fresh, high-quality beans, the proper grind size, and removing the percolator from the heat as soon as the process is complete results in a great pot of coffee for those who enjoy their coffee strong.

There are two types of percolators. One forces boiling water under pressure through the grounds; the other cycles the boiling brew using gravity. The lower section is filled with water, above which is a metal basket that serves as a filter for the ground coffee. Tubing connects the top and bottom sections, and as the temperature rises, the water in the bottom chamber boils, forcing it up the tube.

Boiling water is distributed over the coffee and seeps through the grounds. It continues back into the lower half of the pot, forcing the rest of the colder water up the tube so the whole cycle continuously repeats.

When the overall temperature of the brew reaches the boiling point, the "perking" sound stops, and the coffee is ready for drinking.

camp coffee

Black as the devil. Hot as hell.
Pure as an angel. Sweet as love.

Charles Maurice de Talleyrand-Périgord

t was a week before my wedding day, and, rather than dealing with last-minute details, I was sitting in a cabin in Maine. Called "The Lookout" after the wall of windows that opened onto Baxter State Park's Daicey Pond, I had rented the aging wood structure with the hope of finding some peace before the families made their way north for the ceremony. As my fiancée dozed, I sat in one of the polished log chairs and watched the sun glance early rays off the pond's silent surface. Inspired by the beauty, but also mindful of the early hour, I gathered up the camp stove and a few other necessities, and quietly set about the business of coffee.

There is something positively transcendent about making and drinking a cup of coffee outdoors. It's made all the better because it has no right to be so good. It's dark and grainy, hotter than I normally like; I almost always scald my tongue. Since I'm a bit of a minimalist while camping, I only have a one-cup filter that I pour boiling water through to fill up a small, green plastic cup. I don't think it even makes eight ounces. Nevertheless, there must be something in that river water, or maybe the wind that always scatters the grinds, that makes the experience soul-soothing. Whatever it is, I always look forward to my camp coffee. What I didn't realize that morning in the park was that my future wife had developed a passion for it, too.

I crept softly out onto the cabin porch and had just lit the camp stove—a cantankerous piece of gear if ever there was one—when she came bustling out the door.

"Nope, nope, let me do it!" she cried.

"Yeah, but I like doing it," I replied, somewhat muddled.

"And I like doing it for you. Now go sit down." She bumped me aside and took over.

Before I could say another word, she had taken the coffee, the scoop and my cup, and pushed me bodily off the porch, toward the picnic table. I couldn't believe she was so anxious about it. It wasn't like she was going to drink it. Then again, I should have remembered (and probably would have, had I been given the chance to caffeinate it) that when we first moved in together, the summer after our engagement, my love took it upon herself to make my morning coffee.

At the time, the offer created mixed emotions. On the one hand, I was touched that she would want to serve me in something so important, that she was so anxious to take on this wife's role. On the other hand, I was nervous. This was my coffee we were talking about here. Since I had left home, I had been making it myself, and I was pretty pleased with my abilities. Even at coffee houses, I was usually only begrudgingly satisfied. *Not to mention*, said a tiny voice from the back of my head, *you'll be giving up a piece of control*. On the other hand, I had seen firsthand that marriage could be a battlefield for control. That wasn't what I wanted for us. And, especially amidst a beautiful Maine morning, my pride certainly didn't seem like something worth fighting over. She never expressed any doubt in my coffee-making skills, after all. All she was trying to do was make me happy. If I couldn't let her do that through something like my coffee, what business did I have marrying her?

So it was that when she passed me that steaming cup and kissed me once on the cheek, I turned over the proverbial scoop for good. Since then, I've never asked for it back and never missed it for a moment. It is the pride of my life to know that my wife loves me—mind, body, and coffee-drenched soul.

Chris Bancells

Sunrise Caffè

My heart is twined to your heart
I cannot loosen it now
My song, yours
Through all my light and shadows
My roots go deep and find you there
Where my blossoms wait to be born.

Isabel Bearman Bucher

onna and I were the only true early risers in the family, and we were up before the first pink edges of the dawn began turning a new page. Every morning, it was the same. Up the hill from our house, where I was watching from our small bathroom window, the kitchen screen would squeak. Nonna's head would come snaking around the jam, followed by two thick, waist-length gray braids. Now in her sunrise inspection mode, she'd chirp to a bird or two. A hand would plunge deep into her white chenille robe, which extracted a rumpled paisley hanky. She covered her beak of a nose. Two good honks blasted into the darkness. Dawn agenda complete, she'd disappear into the aroma of her caffè robusta.

That boiled blackness ranked sacred along with St. Mary's Catholic Church holy water and Violette Parfum with which she doused everything she owned. Years later, during a tour of a Catholic Church on the island of Mallorca, the priest stated that violets were the unmistakable scent of the exhumed who were candidates for sainthood. My howl of laughter upset the entire gathering.

I moved soundlessly down the stairs, with Dad's faint snores at my back. Our chiming clock da-da'ed five as I turned the knob of the inner kitchen door and lifted the latch of the mud room exit. I slipped into the dark, moist with morning dew, brimming with the smell of the sea.

"Buongiorno, Nonna," I whispered to her back.

"Good-a morning, Ezabel," she returned softly, her voice registering no surprise.

"Your pronunciation is very good." Without turning, she kept on speaking. "You an early bird. Eh, cara?"

I wanted to tell her I was always up early, pantomiming her, but thought better of it, a bit sheepish and embarrassed.

"I gonna have my caffè now," she stated. "You want a cuppa with me? We watch the sun come up. I tell you stories, eh?"

"Mmmmm," I answered, locking my eyes onto hers. I pictured the thick white mug of steaming, strong coffee, with lots of cream, and three, maybe four spoons of sugar. It was our secret, because if Mamma and Dad knew she was feeding me such black coffee with all that sugar, the lectures about stunting growth would begin, and I'd be cut off from something wonderful. Because Italians were so short, they guarded against anything that would rob them of even one billionth of an inch of height. Nonna was tall for an Italian woman, and she'd been drinking caffè robusta all her life. So much for stunting.

Now seated at the kitchen table, surrounded by chenille and violet scent, I snuggled close, drawing my mug close to my nose. The yellow stove gave silent warmth. Only its softly glowing orange eye coaxed steam from the big coffeepot.

"Ahhh, da caffè's good today!" she purred, taking a huge sniff.

"Ya," I answered, copying her. Da coffee was always good. We continued sipping together, until I tipped the mug and let the sugared bottom trickle slowly into my mouth.

"My Piccolina used to feed me caffè robusta, too," she whispered into my hair, telling me the story about the baby who had been left by Gypsies on her Nonno Luigi's doorstep. "She was the family cook, our head of state in our home in Italy. She live to be a hundred! She bring my Nonna Giudita Anna me caffè every morning, too. Oh, I love-a my Piccolina. You love-a you, Nonna! Eh!"

"Big as the moon," I crooned. "And all the stars and over the rainbow, too!"

"The sun is coming, and you, my bella, my dearest child, you must be going, or else our secret is a secret no more. Eh?"

I rose reluctantly, hugged her middle, inhaling violets one more time, wanting sunrise coffee never to end. "Arrivederci, Mia Nonna," I called back to the screen, giving a backward clasp of the hand that meant "ciao," and moved into the dawn, that palest blue, beribboned with luminous orange. A perfect spider web strung with diamonds began to catch the summoning day, looking for all the world like Nonna's framed handmade lace from some fourteenth-century Italian cathedral.

In the long years since my childhood, I'm not so sure if I became an early riser because I was, or because I longed—needed—to be with Nonna. To wrap in the chenille robe of immensity, her creativity, her wondering, her what-iffing, her magic, her stories that carried forth the push-me-pull-you of our traditions, our language, the stories, and our new adopted ways. What I came to cherish were the solitary times, when two hearts entwine, never to be loosened—a sunrise space when everything normal stops, and learning is everything. That dayspring coffee-with-Nonna space in my heart, with my babies, my husband, my cherished friends, through all the years, has sustained me, uplifted me, gotten me through the very best and worst of times. It's given me the sure knowledge that I could get through any trial, any hardship, of which I've had many, walking strong and sure, due north to a white chenille robe, the sweet smell of violet perfume, and caffè robusta, with three spoons of sugar.

These days, that's where I go when the first ribbons of dawn streak my southwestern sky. I hold my caffè robusta close and whisper, "Da coffee's good today, mia Nonna."

Isabel Bearman Bucher

Firehouse Coffee

Caffeine isn't a drug, it's a vitamin!
Author Unknown

offee on the job is the elixir that keeps things running and firemen fueled, like gasoline for the rigs. On a slow day, it's an excuse for a break from house chores. A chance to forget for just one moment that you could be facing a ten-car pile-up on the freeway in the next. In the middle of a cold winter night, the steaming brew in the white Styrofoam cup handed to you by a kind Red Cross volunteer is what calms the nerves and warms the bones after you've pulled two kids from a burning apartment building. A cuppa joe is what keeps you going when you get back to the station and have the need to sit up and talk about the rescue till dawn.

I got my first lesson in firehouse coffee the morning I started in the department. My Lieutenant at our small north-end station had only one request—"If you don't do anything else around here, kid, learn to make coffee."

Back then it was all percolators, the stovetop variety that gurgled and lifted you up with aroma long before the caffeine hit. I was twenty-four-years old, fresh out of college and eager to fit in with the good ole boy crew at

Station 21. I'd seen my mother make coffee and figured how hard could it be? I watched the Lieutenant spoon fresh grounds with an old shoehorn from the big red can on the counter. He filled the metal basket with twice the amount Mom ever used, then ran the tap water for a full minute "to get out the pipe rust." He placed the filled percolator on the back burner of the old combination stove-refrigerator units that had been salvaged from military surplus and installed in firehouse kitchens.

"The next pot's yours, kid," the Lieutenant grinned and left the room.

Being the obedient rookie they all expected that day, I volunteered for every house chore I could think of, from window washing to replacing urinal cakes. Every time I got the upside-down-mug sign from one of the crew, I'd run to the kitchen and start a fresh pot. The coffee poured out black and thick as mud, just the way the Lieutenant liked it. Nobody argued with his barista technique. After all, he was in charge at Station 21.

By the mid-80s, every station in the city was equipped with drip coffee pots. The rule of thumb was always, "whoever takes the last cup, makes the next pot." Although the managing of coffee was handled differently at each location, you could walk into any station kitchen, any time of day or night, and pour yourself a cup. That is if you could find a cup. Firefighters are a quirky breed— they hoard their coffee cups and stash them the way a ball player might hold on to a favorite glove or bat. More often than not, mugs were hand-rinsed and secreted away in lockers. This strategy also prevented personal cups from falling victim to a firehouse prank.

I learned my second firehouse coffee lesson the hard way—never leave a full cup unattended. There just might be something as strange as a pair of dentures or your missing fire helmet chin strap lurking at the bottom of your cup.

Morning coffee is about the most vital of all firehouse traditions. Whether you've bunked the entire evening or worked a 311 fire all night long, the lure of the brew brings all the troops to the kitchen at the end of a shift. The coffee flows as eagerly as the conversation until the replacement crew arrives to take over. Then you grab your last cup of java for the road and head home.

Don Rogers

The Scoop on Beans

Arabica beans are rich and flavorful. Robusta beans are lower quality, have higher levels of caffeine, and are less flavorful. They are actually two different species of coffee.

Arabicas are more delicate, and are susceptible to pests and vulnerable to temperature and handling. The Arabica species is best when grown at high altitudes. Robustas are much hardier and grow well at lower altitudes in less favorable conditions.

Espresso is often a blend of both, as are lower-priced, commercially available coffees. It takes approximately forty-two coffee beans to make an average serving of espresso.

Ancient Brew

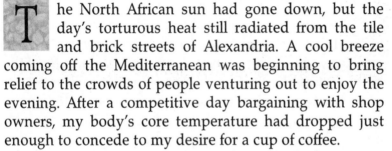

When traveling with someone, take large
doses of patience and tolerance
with your morning coffee.

Helen Hayes

T he North African sun had gone down, but the
day's torturous heat still radiated from the tile
and brick streets of Alexandria. A cool breeze
coming off the Mediterranean was beginning to bring
relief to the crowds of people venturing out to enjoy the
evening. After a competitive day bargaining with shop
owners, my body's core temperature had dropped just
enough to concede to my desire for a cup of coffee.

I was carrying several bags of Egyptian wares as I
passed by prospective coffee shops looking for the
"authentic" local experience. Men sat in dusky nineteenth-
century concrete and stucco shops smoking tobacco, or
sheesha, from water pipes. They sipped on coffee or tea,
talking, reading newspapers, and playing backgammon. I
chose a coffee shop at random and sat down at a small
wooden table on the sidewalk on a fairly busy street
across from a high sea wall and the source of the cool air.

The proprietor of the shop navigated a maze of wooden

tables at which dozens of men were seated. It was his job, in addition to providing drinks, to keep the water pipes burning by refreshing the hot coals and bringing more tobacco when necessary. He sort of swooped in low by my table and took my order on the fly. "Qawha," I said.

"Coffee?" he asked.

"Yes, coffee. Shokran." My attempts at the Arabic language had been few and met with outstanding and friendly English. He disappeared back inside the shop, and I began to relax after my hectic day in the trenches of consumerism. Unable to understand the conversations of the customary all-male clientele, I focused on the cadence, the phrasing and the auditory excitement of the Egyptian evening that accompanied the frenzied pace of the people.

The fast rhythm of dice and clicking ceramic pieces on wooden backgammon tables accompanied the song of the bells of ancient yellow streetcars signaling their presence to the random pedestrian and motor traffic on the street. Silhouettes of the passengers were framed in windows by a dim inner glow, and waves of the great Mediterranean crashed against the sea wall that hid it from view.

The city smelled of spice and sea salt, a natural garnish I would realize after my coffee arrived in a demitasse and I took the first sip. Sweet, thick, grainy and strong, the first taste was an adventure for my palate. Expecting something similar to espresso, I was taken by surprise—this coffee was to be enjoyed over time, not thrown back in a hurry.

As the coffee warmed my soul, I began to see my surroundings with different eyes. I had been very self-conscious all day, and as a tourist I anticipated a certain amount of attention, positive and negative. But in Egypt, as foreign a land as I had ever been to, I had gotten no heavy glares, no awkward scrutiny, no disapproving glances from anybody.

I suddenly felt at home in this city, which had been a crossroads for travelers and traders for millennia, from Cleopatra to Alexander the Great to Napoleon. Why should I attract any attention? I had to laugh out loud as I finished my coffee, leaving a pool of fine grounds in the bottom of the cup.

The waiter gathered the empty demitasse and did not stop to ask how it was. At first, I was disappointed that he left no opening for me to compliment his Qawha, but he knew how good it was. It had always been that way, and whatever I thought was my own business. I began to appreciate that element of the Egyptian culture that was so straightforward. What seemed a moment earlier to be a frenzied pace at which these people lived now seemed to be focused and intentional.

I left the rhythm of the sidewalk for the interior of the coffee shop, curious to see how Qawha is brewed. The high ceiling and muted green tobacco-stained and cracked plaster walls were less than cozy. I approached an aged wooden bar behind which the proprietor was stoking a tiny fire of coals and asked if I could have another coffee. I told him I would like to see how it was brewed, and this made him smile.

He walked over to an ancient stove. The tall back was silver and of a lost age of craftsmanship—beautiful, ornate, and in a high state of polish. The flat stove was covered in several inches of sand that was heated underneath by jets of gas. The hot Saharan sand had been tamed for the use of making coffee—yet another example of man's ability to conquer the elements.

With a proud smile, he began grinding a measure of coffee beans in a hand-operated mill to a texture even finer than that of espresso. He then poured water into an ibrik, a copper vessel with a long wooden handle, followed by sugar and the coffee on top. Soon, the ibrik was surrounded by this hot sand with only the open top sticking out. After several minutes and some skillful manipulation that allowed the coffee to bubble up three times, he poured the contents into a demitasse and slid it across the bar to me.

I raised the tiny cup to him, a craftsman in the ancient and humble art of brewing coffee. It was the best I had ever tasted, earthy and rich, and enjoyed the way it had been for nearly a thousand years.

Sometimes, it can be staggering how small we feel compared to the history of a place, but in the simple moments such as these, while enjoying a cup of coffee, we can find our identity with all people.

Jeremy R. Hope

The Sipping Saucer

See how special you are?
I serve you coffee in the parlor.

Anthony Quinn, The Black Orchid

randma was a lady, no doubt about it. She had not reached that state easily, for she was one of ten children born to dirt-poor, Scots-Irish parents in a rural community of western Illinois. Her daddy supported the family as a small farmer and mailman. He was well-respected, a loving, caring father and husband. He died before Grandma was not a teenager, leaving her mother to struggle financially.

Great-grandfather had built her a loom, and she wove rag rugs to eke out a living for the large family. She and Grandma's older brothers wanted her to have a better life, so Grandma was sent to live a while with an aunt who had married well in Springfield. It was from this aunt that Grandma was to learn "town ways" and good manners. She was always conscious of what a gift this experience was, for it did lead to a better life, and eventually marriage to an up-and-coming, young dental surgeon.

"Behave like FOLKS!" she would admonish me, just as her aunt had said to her. And, like her, I was sent away during the Great Depression years when my father could not find work. How blessed I was that it was to live with Grandma and my grandfather. It was largely from Grandma that I, too, learned to mind my manners. Grandma was a wonderful companion to me as a small child, and I was totally happy in her comfortably large home. But Grandma was a stickler for doing things the proper way. So it always seemed peculiar to me that she drank her morning coffee out of a saucer! She made a pot of coffee every morning in a stove-top percolator, and it smelled heavenly to me. I longed to try it, but Grandma said it would stunt my growth! Sometimes she added a few pieces of eggshell to the pot—I had no idea why, but other folks did as well in those days. Except on school days, breakfast was a leisurely affair. While the coffee percolated, Grandma fried herself two eggs and one for me, and made us toast that she liberally slathered with home-made grape jelly.

We enjoyed our breakfast at the kitchen table that was brightly covered with a red checked oilcloth. She would pour herself a cup of coffee, and in a few minutes, would lift the cup from the saucer below and pour coffee into the saucer. Then, with both hands, she gracefully raised the saucer to her lips to drink. When I privately asked my grandfather why Grandma drank her coffee that way, he said it was to avoid getting her mouth burned. That made sense, so I never questioned it. But as I grew older, and Grandma became more adamant about good manners, I began to feel a little embarrassed by her saucer sipping because it was obvious that other people whom we respected drank from their cups.

When I was about twelve, I was allowed to have a friend from school come spend a weekend with us. I was a little nervous, as her mother was one of my teachers and a very proper lady herself. I did not know Dorothy very well, but hoped we would become best friends. I wanted the weekend to be special and to impress her. All was fine Friday evening when she came. Grandma's dinner, as always, was something to be proud of. Afterward, we were permitted to have Coca-Colas, but Grandma would not let me serve Dorothy from a bottle of Coke. "That's not good manners," Grandma said, setting out glasses for us. Kids everywhere drank Coke from bottles, I protested in vain.

It was Saturday morning, though, when I felt anxious. Grandma was at the breakfast table when we girls got up. We came into the kitchen, and there sat Grandma calmly drinking her coffee from a saucer as she read the morning paper. Grandma got up and fixed us a special breakfast of pancakes and sausages. I was happy until she sat down again and joined us, pouring out some coffee into her saucer and sipping daintily from it as always, her elbows on the table to steady the saucer. I wanted to sink right down in my chair and slide under the table. My face was hot with embarrassment.

What would Dorothy think? Would she ever want to come back to our house? Would she think Grandma a dumb old country woman who didn't know any better? She was watching Grandma's every move—the way she poured fresh, steaming coffee into her cup, then from the cup to the saucer, and then carefully lifting it to savor the aroma and slowly drink it.

After we ate, Grandma sent us outside to play, telling us we didn't have to help wash the dishes. I was glad to escape, yet dreading what Dorothy would say when we were out of earshot. She looked at me, and I stood very still, waiting for the worst. Perhaps she would want to go home right away and never be my friend.

"Marcia," Dorothy said with a sigh, "I just love your grandma! My grandmother never makes pancakes. And isn't yours just the sweetest thing? Doesn't she have lovely hands? I never saw anyone drink coffee so gracefully." I was stunned. And ashamed of myself. I wanted more than ever to be friends with this girl who saw only beauty in a loving old woman sipping coffee from a saucer. And I was never embarrassed by Grandma's ways again.

Marcia E. Brown

A New Reason to Exercise

The powers of a man's mind are directly
proportioned to the quantity
of coffee he drinks.

Sir James Mackintosh

or years I have struggled to be regular in my fitness routine. I know I should exercise more, which is why I joined a gym in the first place. Unfortunately, joining the gym didn't automatically get me to the gym. So I came up with what I thought was a sure-fire way to keep my fitness goals on track.

Plan One: Arise early in the morning, drive directly to the gym, work out for an hour, shower, and be finished by 9:00 or 10:00 AM. Unfortunately, I was only able to keep that up for a month. You see, I started in September, and living in Oregon means that October brings many weather changes that were not conducive to my commitment. I would find myself lying in bed listening to the rain pelting on the windows, the wind howling through the fir trees, and I'd feel myself sinking deeper and deeper into the mattress as the down comforter seemed to whisper sweetly in my ear, "Go back to sleep. You can always go to the gym tomorrow morning when the weather's better."

Sadly, the next day was strangely like the last, and my goal to work out in the mornings slowly faded away.

But I'm a determined woman, and where there's a will, there must be a way . . . but which way? I became convinced that since mornings didn't work, surely evenings would be better. I would have had all the sleep I needed, I would be done with all the chores and shopping, so I could just drive myself right over to that gym and join an aerobics class. Unfortunately, I had forgotten how early it gets dark here in the Northwest. I also realized that most of the evening classes were filled with young, athletic, and energetic people, so after a few pitiful attempts to stay and work out, I resigned myself to my fiftyish age and stayed home where I was safe and sound.

By now I was becoming extremely frustrated and angry with myself. Weight was gaining on me, and the newspapers were screaming at me: weight gain leads to high blood pressure, diabetes, heart disease, etc. . . . . Plus, the money I had to pay each month for the gym that I didn't use was beginning to make me feel so guilty that I was eating my way through my kitchen.

That is, until that fateful day when I opened the morning newspaper and, to my surprise and delight, was greeted with the headlines that would forever change my attitude toward exercise: "New Studies Prove Chocolate and Caffeine Provide Health Benefits."

As I began to read, I found that science had finally caught up with the knowledge that women have known for centuries: chocolate and caffeine are actually good for you. They even provide antioxidants that help correct everything from Alzheimer's to high blood pressure!

What joy I felt as I packed my gym bag as quickly as I could and headed to the gym. I worked out with renewed determination for over an hour. Later, as I sat at a table in Starbucks sipping my non-fat mocha, I relished my new-found reward for keeping my appointment to exercise. That was over four years ago.

Exercising consistently has changed my life in so many ways. I feel healthier, not only physically, but also emotionally. And going to the gym on a regular basis has allowed me to meet other women who struggle with a reason to exercise. So now I am no longer alone at Starbucks, but meet with others who have taken the pledge to keep on exercising and enjoying their chocolate and caffeine . . . for medicinal purposes, of course.

Patricia Hoyt

Ways to Brew the Bean: Drip

By far the most common way to prepare coffee in the United States is the drip method.

Nearly boiled water is poured over medium-coarse ground coffee. The drip method requires a filter—disposable paper or permanent metal and plastic are available. The paper filter will trap some of the flavorful oils in your coffee, and many coffee lovers feel a plastic filter imparts an off-taste, so metal is generally preferred.

You'll need a finer grind for paper filters and a slightly coarser grind for permanent filters.

cheese and coffee

Good communication is as stimulating as
black coffee, and just as hard to sleep after.

Anne Morrow Lindbergh

y son Shane has a friend who is so quiet that I knew him for two years before I discovered his real name. When I saw him, I would wave, and the boy I knew as "Cheese" would nod and look away, his long hair covering a strikingly handsome face.

"What's the story with Cheese?" I asked my son.

"What do you mean?" He was never too anxious to give up more than essential facts to his mother.

"I mean, tell me about him."

"I dunno; Cheese is Cheese. He's cool."

"What is his real name?"

"He's got a German name . . . Louden, Latten . . . something."

"Do you have any classes with him? Is he a good student?"

"He's really quiet, but smart, Mom. He's not doing drugs, running a prostitution ring or robbing people after school, okay?" I knew I had begun to interrogate, so I backed off.

I guess it is a mother's instinct to want to know the kind of people her children are spending time with when they are not at home. You hear stories of teenagers getting in with the wrong crowd and mothers lamenting that their children wouldn't act out alone . . . that friends had changed them. I didn't have a bad feeling about Cheese; I just felt uneasy that I didn't know him. He seemed to be keeping his distance.

Nonetheless, he came to every event my son attended, and after a few months of waving to him, I was surprised when one day he not only waved back but smiled. My son ran to the car. "There's a party at Cheese's this weekend. Can I go?"

"Will his parents be there?"

"Cheese! Supervised?" my son yelled. Cheese held up two fingers and wiggled them.

"He says both parents will be there."

"Okay, I'll get the particulars later." I felt apprehensive. We had lived in the city for only a year. This would be my son's first high-school party, and I knew nothing about the host. He could be into pornography, computer hacking, or drugs. You know what they say . . . it's always the quiet ones.

My fears were unfounded. The party was a success, and Shane returned unharmed and told me about nearly every minute of the night. Cheese continued to smile when he waved.

A few months later, Shane asked if he could invite Cheese over along with their mutual friend, Emily, to play video games. I thought it would be a good way to get to know my son's friend, so I agreed. I already knew Emily. She was a ball of sunshine, and I looked forward to her visits. She was very entertaining and easy to get along with.

In fact, with Emily around, no one else has to talk as she keeps things hopping!

Both kids arrived, and Cheese's mother nodded as she turned her car to leave. It occurred to me that I had seen that same nod in her son. One mystery solved.

The teenagers disappeared into the barn where loud music soon emanated. I peeked in from time to time, but left them to their conversations, music, and video games.

Emily came in to pick up snacks.

"What's going on with you guys?" I asked.

"Nothing. You know boys, absolutely nothing." She shook her head and disappeared with chips and drinks.

When the hour grew late, Shane came into our office just as I was about to go find him. "Can they please spend the night?" I looked at my calendar; nothing planned for Saturday morning.

"If it's okay with their parents, it's okay with me." His face relaxed with relief.

"They say it's okay." He ran off before I could berate him for planning without asking in advance. The kids came inside and resumed video games until the wee hours of the morning.

I went to bed, awoke at the usual hour, and headed to the kitchen where the automatic coffeepot had a full pot waiting for me. I sat with my brew until I heard unfamiliar footsteps approaching.

"Hey." It was Cheese. My first word from him!

"Good morning. Did you sleep all right?"

"Yeah," he said, and he glanced at the coffee in my hand before turning to walk away.

"Would you like a cup of coffee?" He turned around and smiled.

"That would be good." A sentence! I handed him a cup, and pointed him toward the cream and sugar, which he refused.

"I like it black, thanks."

I have a theory about people who drink black coffee. They don't need accoutrements because they value the essentials.

My grandfather was the first person I knew who drank his coffee black. He was a listener and a man of few words, but when he spoke everyone listened. He didn't care much for extras, didn't display his emotions overtly, and when greeting someone for the first time, he always nodded.

"What's your first name, Cheese?" I asked, aware that if he was like my grandfather, he might not be shy at all, just efficient.

"Kevan Lautenschlager."

"It's nice to meet you, Kevan. I'm Dawn." He grinned at the silliness of the late introduction, but as he put his coffee to his lips, I saw the same long nasal inhalation my grandfather used to draw in his coffee before drinking it. I suddenly felt I knew this quiet kid and loved him.

As I had often done with my grandfather, I wracked my brain for an efficient sentence to get the right information without being dismissed as foolish.

"What are you planning to study in college?" came out.

"Biology and botany." He looked into his coffee as if preparing an answer to the inevitable next question.

"Why?"

"Because plants have a profound impact on human life. Not many people realize that they are useful far beyond food and furniture." I was intrigued; my face must have shown it.

"Have you ever heard of the Datura plant?" he said.

"The hallucinogenic weed from Don Juan?" His eyes opened as if he had seen me for the first time.

"Not just a hallucinogen. Datura was used as a pain-killer and a sedative, but it's also a deadly poison!"

"How would you know that?"

"I read a lot about plants. Did you know this coffee we are drinking used to be for-bidden by the Muslim reli-gion? They said it was intoxicating. Coffee has been used to successfully treat diabetes, cirrhosis of the liver, and asthma in babies."

"I had no idea."

Kevan related more about the plants he had studied. All of his information was new to me.

As we were finishing a second cup, Shane and Emily walked into the kitchen and stared in wonder that Kevan was talking. Neither drinks coffee so it was a while before they awakened, and they just sat in fascination, as I did, at

The Daily Grind

There are different types of grinders, the most common being a blade grinder. Two metal blades spin at very high speeds to chop and crush the coffee bean.

To produce a more uniform grind of bean, a burr (or milling) grinder can be used. The benefit of a uniform grind is a more flavorful coffee. Within the burr-grinding family are flat and conical burr models, but for the average consumer it's simply a matter of preference as to which to purchase.

the openness a simple cup of coffee had awakened.

When the conversation shifted to the day's activities, Kevan grew quiet again and allowed the others to make plans. When they left, Kevan turned and waved. I smiled and nodded over my third cup.

I've never called him Cheese since.

Dawn Howard

Campfire Coffee—Nothing Better!

There is nothing like being left alone again,
to walk peacefully with oneself in the woods.
To boil one's coffee and fill one's pipe, and
to think idly and slowly as one does it.

Knut Hamsun

y morning assignment at the campsite was to make the coffee, which should have been no problem.

I'd been fixing coffee since I was old enough to drink it. In my family, that meant ten or eleven years old. I mastered my mother's Crazy Daisy electric percolator when I still had to stand on a stepstool to reach it. For my sixteenth birthday, my grandmother gave me my very own Mister Coffee machine, still one of my favorite presents of all time.

Whether brewed or perked, the coffee I made was always delicious. Everybody said so. But my campfire coffee was the best. What could compare to the aroma and taste of coffee fixed in the great outdoors, served scalding hot in speckled tin mugs with a spoonful of sugar and a splash of real cream?

Nothing in this world.

My husband George and I honeymooned in a campground in the Great Smoky Mountains National Park. It was there that he taught me to gather dead twigs and to arrange them tepee-style over a pile of dry leaves in the middle of the fire ring. He showed me how to add bigger sticks once the kindling had caught and to put real logs on the flame at exactly the right time.

But I'm the one who taught him to set the aluminum coffeepot—a wedding present from my sister—on just the right spot on the fire grate so that it would percolate but not boil. I showed him how to use kitchen tongs to remove the filter basket so we didn't wind up with coffee grounds in our mugs. And I'm the one who persuaded him that it was a sin to wait for coffee to cool before drinking it.

"The hotter the better," I told him, swilling mine down with a satisfied smile the instant it was poured.

Camping became one of our favorite hobbies. On our fifth wedding anniversary, I surprised George with a "screen house"—a tall tent with see-through sides that could be used as a campsite kitchen. Rain, insects, skunks, and raccoons would no longer wreak havoc on our cooking and eating.

His gift to me was equally exciting—a two-burner Coleman camp stove. "Coffee, bacon and eggs, hamburgers—you name it, we can cook it on this stove," he said with a grin.

We invited a couple who were close friends and equally enthusiastic about the outdoors to accompany us to the mountains a couple of weekends later. Like George, they were avid fishermen. But not me. Especially not at 4:30 AM when they planned to depart for the trout stream.

"I'll just sleep in," I told them. "At least until sunrise. As long as the firewood stays dry, I'll have a pot of coffee waiting for you when you get back."

"How soon you forget, my sweet," George said, shaking his head in feigned disappointment. "No need for campfire coffee anymore now that we have a stove."

"But I don't have any idea how to work that thing," I told him.

"It's easy," he said, placing the camp stove on the table in the center of the screen house. "First, flip this lever over. Then pump up the fuel tank pressure valve like so. Now, all you have to do is twist this black knob just a little." He pointed to it. "Hold the lighter to the burner and, voilà, you're cooking with gas."

"Gee, honey, I don't know. Maybe I better not fool with the stove till you get back."

"Suit yourself. But we're low on firewood, and it may be late into the morning before we're finished fishing. You know how you get if you have to wait that long for coffee."

He was right. I couldn't bear the thought of three or four hours without my magic morning elixir. Okay, okay. I'd make camp-stove coffee. How hard could it be?

The sky was threatening rain when I crawled out of the tent the next morning shortly after dawn. George and our friends had been gone for a couple of hours. I figured that the thunder rumbling in the west would drive them back to the campsite soon.

I'd better get started on the coffee, I told myself.

I tramped over to the campground's lone water spigot and filled the coffeepot, now dented and stained after five years of hard use, with cold water. I carried it back to the screen house and carefully measured just the right amount of grounds into the basket. I set it atop the stem and snapped the lid into place, just as I'd done dozens of times before.

Then it was time to light the stove. Flip the lever over, I reminded myself. Pump the fuel pressure valve. No problem so far. But next came the part that made me nervous—putting flame to gas.

George had told me to twist the black knob and hold the lighter to the burner. But how far was I supposed to twist it? I couldn't remember. I tried a quarter turn and struck the lighter to life. The burner wouldn't catch. I turned the knob a little more.

Still nothing. Perhaps he'd said to open it up all the way while I was lighting and then turn it down before I put on the coffeepot.

Yes, that must be what I was supposed to do.

WHOOSH! The second the spark from the lighter came in contact with all that gas, a gigantic ball of flame leapt from the stove, engulfing the plastic roof of the screen house, which immediately began to melt.

"Help!" I hollered, running toward the tent in the next campsite. "Fire! Help!"

In no time at all, dozens of fellow campers came to my rescue, tossing buckets of water onto the screen house that now lay flattened and smoldering on the ground. Then, mercifully, rain began falling in sheets. The fire would not spread. I thanked those who had helped me and crawled meekly back into my tent to wait out the storm. There would be no coffee at our campsite that morning. And I knew what present I would ask my sister for at Christmas—a new aluminum coffeepot to replace the one that had just burned to smithereens.

Jennie Ivey

Decadent Treats—Not for the Purist

Chocolate-covered coffee beans: Melt dark semi-sweet chocolate. Cover a baking sheet with wax paper. Spread dark roasted beans on the baking sheet. Pour the melted chocolate over the beans and cover them well. Spread them into a single layer and put the sheet in the refrigerator. When it's solid, break into pieces.

Quick and easy mocha: Add chocolate syrup or hot chocolate mix to espresso or a dark-roasted coffee.

Perked up: Drop an Altoid—yes, the breath mint—in with your coffee when brewing to make a delicious, easy peppermint coffee. Substitute a bit of cinnamon if you prefer that flavor.

Nuts about coffee: For a more subtle flavor than syrups, grind your favorite nut and sprinkle it in the coffee when brewing. Hazelnut, almond, and macadamia all taste wonderful.

A Cup of Black Coffee

Do I like my coffee black?
There are other colors?

Author Unknown

 hat is enlightenment? I say that it is a spiritual awakening. And that it can be brought about by simple things like sipping black coffee out of a gold-trimmed, porcelain cup.

I am a known tea drinker, and I always drank my tea thick, milky, somewhat sweet, steaming hot, and straight from a glass. It had to conform to these rather stringent standards, just like everything else that mattered in my life.

Here I was then, suddenly holding a cup of black coffee without sugar, sitting alone under the sun on a Parisian boulevard. For me, the black coffee symbolized a rite of passage. The sweetness had disappeared from my life sometime ago, and the coffee was telling in its blackness. I had traveled to France and realized that black coffee was what was drunk by the very sexy and slim French. All of a sudden, I wanted to be like them.

All in all, I was an Indian hausfrau suddenly coming to terms with my humdrum existence and deciding that drinking black coffee would be the first taste in the right direction.

I had to travel to Paris to understand this. It may make you laugh or shake your head. You could have drunk coffee in your back yard, you'd probably say, and remained as slim as the French and kept the sweetness in your life as well. But that would never have occurred to me. And I don't think it would have worked either.

I had never drunk black coffee before, and I would never have gone near it at home. I had no penchant for coffee till then. But in Paris, I decided to give it a try. As I stared down at the swirling black concoction within the cup and inhaled the hot, stimulating aroma, I felt myself changing from within. Then I took a tentative sip. The coffee was so different; it made me feel different. I think I felt more alive.

Sometimes you just need that extra kick to move your life into gear, and it had to be black coffee in Paris to do it for me.

I sipped and watched the birds wheeling in delight over the waters of the Seine in the autumn sun. A dry red-gold leaf skittered in the wind and disappeared. A couple walked past me in their low-slung jeans upheld by wide leather belts, their sweaters tight against their young chests. Only the slight swell of the girl's bust revealed her sex. Another couple walked past, their arms around each other, and both of them had yesterday's unshaved beard. I did not blink an eye. The magic of coffee was working. I could see and accept things in a world different from mine.

It is strange that sitting there I found the answer to

some of my questions. At home in India, despite the appearance of being a liberated woman, I had been in a stifling environment for so long that I had begun to think that was all my life was about. Stepping out of my cocooned existence and leaving for France was a big step forward for me and required a lot of guts. I left because I needed to see the world, and a fire was burning in my stomach.

The sip of coffee only ignited it further. I needed now to see more, to find out about how other people lived, to break the monotonous confines of my previous life. I also needed to tell people how important it was to step out of one's back yard.

Wondrous change takes place when we are exposed to the sights, sounds, culture, habits, and thinking of people other than our own, when we decide to spread our wings and try different things.

Enlightenment comes in many forms. Sometimes it just takes a cup of black coffee.

Abha Iyengar

Lessons in a Cup of Coffee

Work becomes easier, and you will sit down
without distress to your principal repast,
which will restore your body
and afford you a calm, delicious night.

Charles Maurice de Talleyrand-Perigord

or me, drinking coffee marked the dividing line between being a kid and being an adult. So, when I started drinking coffee the summer I turned seventeen, I considered myself grown up. Every morning, I'd stumble out of bed, pour myself a large cup from the pot my mother made, and let the aroma of the dark, rich liquid coax me awake. No matter how hot the day, I began it with a cup of coffee.

That was the same summer I worked as a part-time volunteer in the coffee shop at a rehabilitation hospital. My job entailed standing behind the counter and working the coffee machine. "It's an easy job," Jeanne, the paid worker, said. "Change the filters for every new pot, fill them with the pre-measured packs of ground coffee, keep the empty pots on the back burners, and smile at the customers. You'll do fine." She was only half right.

Making the coffee was easy; serving the customers

proved harder. I quickly got used to patients with crutches, walkers, and artificial limbs. However, burn patients, with their bodies, hands or faces covered in angry scar tissue, were almost more than I could bear. One of the regulars had burns along the right side of his face. Raw, puckered skin ran from his forehead to his jaw, twisting his mouth. The first time Luc came in, after the lunch crowd had left, I had just poured myself a cup of coffee. I glanced up at the sound of footsteps nearing my station, and even more quickly glanced away. I fussed with coffeepots that didn't need attention, turned cup handles to face the same direction, and straightened sugar envelopes—all to avoid looking directly at him.

"Coffee," he grunted, his voice harsh. I nodded, filled a cup, and held it out for him—not meeting his gaze. When he didn't take the cup, I finally looked up. He held up two bandaged hands and gave me a lopsided smile.

"No problem," I murmured, my face hot.

"Have a seat. I'll bring the coffee over." I came around the other side of the counter, got his coffee, and followed him to a table set off in a corner. As I placed the coffee in front of him, I wondered how he'd manage to drink it. He put both hands around the cup and very slowly and carefully raised it to his mouth, without spilling a drop. He took one sip, sighed, and put the cup back down, just as slowly and carefully. I went back to my station at the coffeepots and occasionally glanced in his direction while I drank my own coffee. He sat for about half an hour, then left.

When I cleaned his table, his cup remained almost full. Luc returned every afternoon at 2:00 PM. By the second week, I could look at him directly. By the third week, I could smile at him. By the fourth week, my smile reflected a genuine welcome, and we chatted a little. During the fifth week, since he came at a quiet time, I timed my break to coincide with his arrival. I brought two cups of coffee to the table and sat down with him. At first, we talked about the weather, the news, unimportant things. Later, we talked about ourselves. Just ten years older than me, he told me about his family and his work, though he never spoke about how he got so badly burned. I told him about my plans to attend university in the fall and confided that I was unsure what I wanted to study.

His voice remained harsh, but his facial burns were a little less angry, and the bandages on his hands weren't as thick. Yet even as he improved, he continued to take just one sip of his coffee. When I asked him why, he said he didn't really like coffee. "But you come here and order coffee every day," I said.

He shrugged before answering. "When I first came to the hospital, I hid in my room. Who would want to look at me? After a few weeks, the doctor told me I had to go to the coffee shop as part of my therapy to get used to people looking at my face."

"I'm sorry," I whispered, thinking back to my own reaction the first time I saw him.

He patted my hand gently. "We both had a hard time at first. But it's better now. Right?"

I nodded, blinking away tears. My last day at work, Luc didn't come in. I asked Jeanne if she knew anything about him.

"I forgot," she said. "The doctor released him this morning, much earlier than expected. He'll be an outpatient now. He came in a few hours ago to say good-bye, but I told him you only work afternoons."

I nodded, disappointed, and returned to my station. I spent my last afternoon making fresh pots of coffee and filling cups. I also polished every surface of the coffee machine until it shone. Every so often, I'd glance at the empty table, surprised at how much I missed his company. The afternoon dragged, but five o'clock finally arrived. As my last act, I poured myself a cup of coffee and brought it over to Luc's table. I sat there for a few minutes and took one sip. Then to complete the ritual, I returned the cup to the counter, poured out the remaining coffee, and washed the cup.

When I think about that summer, over thirty years ago, I remember the deep, rich smell of coffee and Luc, the man with the burned face. I was wrong about one important thing, though. Drinking coffee didn't make me a grown-up; learning to see beyond the surface of someone's skin did.

Harriet Cooper

Ways to Brew the Bean:
Vacuum (or Vac Pot or Siphon Brewer)

Widely popular in the United States until the automatic-drip coffee maker was invented, many consider vacuum brewing the best way to make a great-tasting pot of coffee. It's also fascinating.

This infusion method takes longer and may seem complicated, but once you get the hang of it, the process is simple. Delicate coffees are suited for vacuum brewing. It produces a thinner cup of coffee without the sediment you get in other brewing methods.

Vacuum brewers consist of two spheres. The top holds the coffee and filter; the bottom holds the water. They are connected by a siphon tube. A medium to fine grind works best in a ratio of about two rounded (not heaping) tablespoons per six ounces of water.

The pot is placed over medium heat, and as the heated water rises up, it blends with the coffee grounds. After the coffee brews for 2–3 minutes, the pot is removed from the stove. Without its heat source, a vacuum is created, forcing the coffee to trickle back down through the filter, down the siphon tube, and through the spent grounds. Finishing is often heralded by a bubbling action in the bottom globe for a few seconds as air is pulled through the spent grounds.

Usually, the entire process takes about twelve minutes, including heating the water, brewing, and finishing.

Served with Honor

Conscience keeps more people
awake than coffee.

Author Unknown

ome people drink coffee only in the morning, some only with meals, and others drink coffee all day long. Working as the hostess in our family-owned restaurant, I became acquainted with all of them, but I really got to know the regulars on a very personal level.

At our restaurant, if you bought a cup of coffee, you paid for one cup and drank as many refills as you liked. The regular coffee drinkers were men who congregated at the same table every day. Buck was a regular who became family. He came and went throughout the day, whenever he felt the need for a caffeine fix or a little friendly conversation.

I saw past Buck's need for a cup of hot coffee and listened attentively when he began to open up and talk to me. I sat when business was slow, enjoying his company. He reminded me of my dad, who had also served in World War II, and I encouraged him to share his memories of the war.

At first, Buck was reluctant, but as he warmed up to me,

he told me about landing on Omaha Beach and how some of his fellow soldiers never made it to shore. Tears glistened in his eyes, or was it the steam from his coffee cup? As he talked, I filled his cup. I encouraged, praised, and was in awe of this humble man who had guided tanks through villages. One day, he trusted me enough to reveal the fear that had gripped him when bullets went clean through his helmet. Stories he'd never told before surfaced as we sat together.

The coffeepot continued to drip, the brewing aroma like a warm cocoon that wrapped our conversations in a rare friendship. Buck was an old warrior who was fortunate to return home when many died and others faced the guilt of having survived. Eventually, I began to see Buck's chest swell with pride for the things I admired about him.

The day Buck missed stopping in for his usual coffee, his wife phoned with word that Buck had passed. The regulars' table was never quite the same again.

I am proud to have called Buck my friend, and I am honored that the simple act of filling his coffee cup gave me the opportunity to show him my admiration, validate his bravery, and provide a release from his pain held inside for much too long.

Betty King

2

TICKLING THE TASTEBUDS

An Unexpected Secret Ingredient

A fig for partridges and quails,
ye dainties I know nothing of ye;
But on the highest mount in Wales
Would choose in peace to drink my coffee.

Jonathan Swift

y head buzzed with anticipation and anxiety as I rang the doorbell of a handsome two-story brick house. A chill passed through me, and I crossed my arms against the breeze that blew in from the west, the air thick with the scent of salt water and the cries of sea gulls. This was the moment I had anticipated for months with both anxiety and excitement. Almost two years into my relationship with a young man named Emmett O'Connor, our parents would finally meet for the first time.

The delay in their meeting was due not to their objection to Emmett's and my romance, but rather to distance. For the past two years, I had been attending graduate school in Galway, on the west coast of Ireland. As my parents and I waited at the door for a moment, I turned to give them an encouraging smile. They looked as nervous as I felt, and I prayed our families would get along well.

Although the O'Connor house had become nearly as

familiar to me as my own childhood home, I continued to marvel at its surroundings. To reach the small village of Barna, we had driven west out of Galway City along Galway Bay, passing new housing developments nestled into lush green hillsides. Suburban neighborhoods soon gave way to sloping landscapes that touched the rocky coastline. Emmett's family home was set along the coast, where winter winds pummeled the house, and the sounds of traffic along the main road were often drowned out by whipping rain.

But this was a glorious spring day; bright and cool, the wind mercifully still. I rang the bell again. Within seconds, Emmett's father was at the door, inviting us in. Introductions were made. Everyone was polite but seemed unsure how to bridge the distance between the backgrounds and cultures of these two families. Usually in Ireland, friendships were built over pots of tea, carefully brewed according to traditional rituals.

During visits with our relations in Ireland, my mother had politely accepted delicate cups of strong Irish tea, often sweetening it with spoonfuls of sugar. But she was a coffee-drinking woman, and I suspected she longed for the familiarity and flavor of a large mug of good black coffee. I'd been an avid coffee drinker myself when I'd arrived in the country. While I still enjoyed a cup of coffee each morning, I'd grown accustomed to ordering a pot of tea in cafés and restaurants. My roommate and I shared a pot of tea each evening, and when friends stopped by for a chat, it was always tea that we made to share.

So as we settled into the O'Connors' cozy, modern

kitchen, Emmett's father asked a question that seemed to set my mother immediately at ease. "Would anyone care for a cup of coffee?" Mom's hand shot up. Most of the coffee served in Irish cafés and restaurants was drinkable, but unremarkable. Although both Mom and I took our coffee black, we often added milk in Ireland, just to give the coffee some body. I'd made coffee for her in my apartment, but it must have been average as well, since she never commented on it either way.

I'd had many cups of what I'd come to refer to as Mr. O'Connor's "Barna Coffee," named after the village where they lived. I knew it would be superior to the coffee Mom had previously encountered in Ireland. She watched as Mr. O'Connor took down a mug and placed a plastic filter directly on top. Water was boiled in an electric kettle and then poured through the coffee grounds in the filter. The coffee was then allowed to rest so the flavor would be absorbed. Mr. O'Connor also used a secret ingredient—a small dash of sea salt thrown into the filter with the coffee grounds. The salt enhanced the coffee's bold, nutty flavor, but it also did something even more abstract and significant. Sea salt produced a cup of coffee that itself contained part of the mystical, romantic surroundings that had become my home.

With the element of salt from the sea, Barna Coffee evoked not only the salt air and wind of the West of Ireland, but also the play of light and color in the mountains of County Clare across the bay. It evoked the patterns created on ancient oaks by sunlight spilling through the trees in Barna Woods. It brought to mind the cold, gray days when I stood watching the horses graze in the field down the road. With one sip, I knew my mom was as captivated as I was—not just with Barna Coffee, but with all its ingredients, both elemental and magical.

"I'm sorry, Mary," she said. "The coffee you've made for me has been fine. But this is the best coffee I've ever had."

The simple act of sharing a full-bodied cup of coffee enabled my parents and Emmett's parents to find common ground in other areas, and they spent the rest of the afternoon chatting easily. And from then on, our title for Best Coffee in the World went not to a rich Italian espresso or robust French brew, but to a cup of coffee prepared with the most fundamental of local ingredients and served in an unassuming house along the windswept Irish coast.

Mary Caffrey Knapke

"I'm not concerned that coffee will keep me awake all night. I have credit card problems that do that for me."

Obituary Notice

Longtime Soldotna resident, Mister Coffee (Model # 05321) died of unknown causes on Thursday, May 18, 2006, while his family peacefully overslept.

Mister Coffee was manufactured in China and distributed from Cleveland, Ohio, in 1990. From there, he traveled to Juneau, Alaska, where he was purchased via a local retail outlet by the Michels family. On June 15, 1990, Mister Coffee began his lifetime career as Head of Household—Coffeemaker Extraordinaire.

In 1995, Mister Coffee accompanied the Michels family to the Kenai Peninsula. The family fondly recalls that Mister Coffee averaged two pots of coffee per day, and has, over the course of his lifetime, produced over eleven thousand, nine hundred and fifty perfect cups of coffee.

Gifted with a handsome, spill-proof, stainless-steel insulated carafe, Mister Coffee never burnt a single cup of coffee. The family noted that Mister Coffee heroically exceeded his one-year warranty and faithfully performed his duties without requiring service of any kind.

During his lifetime, Mister Coffee's insulated carafe has carried and dispensed many fine blends of coffee. Besides accompanying the family to numerous sporting events, Mister Coffee's sidekick enjoyed many adventures and scenic drives throughout the state of Alaska, parts of Canada, and the lower "forty eight."

Mister Coffee is survived by a Mister Coffee FT Series semi-automatic (professional model), by his family, and by longtime acquaintances: the Kenmore Washer and Dryer Couple, Mr. Kirby, as well as numerous counter mates and fellow appliances, and his domestic partner, La Petite Espresso Machine.

Mister Coffee was preceded in his demise by a $19.95 Norelco Slice O' Matic, a 1975 avocado-green dishwasher, two cordless phones, and a generic blender.

Per Mister Coffee's request, a celebration of his longevity will be held on June 15, 2006, at 5:30 AM at the Michels residence. His grounds will be scattered into the family's compost pile, and his last pot of coffee will be boiled and poured out as a burnt offering to the espresso goddess "Caffinedra."

Family and friends are welcome to attend, provided that they bring doughnuts, paper cups and condiments.

In lieu of flowers, the family requests a large bag of organic beans and a Thermos.

Donations will be gladly accepted at the Displaced Coffeemaker's Institute or repair shop of your choice.

Jacqueline J. Michels

A Cup of Christmas

It is the duty of all papas and mammas to
forbid their children to drink coffee, unless
they wish to have little dried-up machines,
stunted and old at the age of twenty.

Jean Anthelme Brillat-Savarin

My mom is a coffee drinker. I say this the way someone might describe another person as tall or a marathon runner. It's an indisputable fact. She first started drinking coffee as a child of maybe nine or ten—a good thing, since coffee is supposed to stunt your growth, and she ended up being 5'9".

As a devoted coffee drinker, my mom is very particular about her brew. Not instant. Not the flavored varieties that I tend to favor. Just regular coffee. And the coffee-drinking experience is crucial to her enjoyment. Over the years, there are some rules that have developed that we studiously follow.

The coffee must be purchased at independent coffee houses, not chains, and only if a diner, bakery, or café is not available. It matters what the coffee is served in—a ceramic or glass mug that has some weight to it, something that fits nicely in your cupped palms. Styrofoam is definitely out. The option of a free second cup definitely carries weight. In fact, some of the longest moments of my childhood were the hours between when I finished gulping my chocolate milk and waiting for my mom to slowly sip the last drops of her second cup of coffee.

Genetics is a funny thing. My father and brother drink coffee, and by all rights, I should too, especially given the time I spend scouting out places for coffee in preparation for my mom's visits. Coffee is just not my thing, or at least, it didn't used to be. But then one Christmas holiday when I was in my twenties, my mom and I found ourselves in a coffee house after an afternoon of shopping.

"What would you like?" she asked.

"What?"

"You need to get something."

"Oh." Apparently, there was a new rule—don't drink coffee alone.

I pursed my lips and studied the menu. Tea at restaurants is horribly expensive and, I've learned the hard way, is usually way too hot to actually drink. Apple cider and hot chocolate made me feel like a little kid. And then I saw the holiday specials—coffees flavored

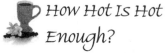

How Hot Is Hot Enough?

The best water temperature for coffee is about 205°F.

Colder water doesn't extract enough of the oils from the beans, and hotter water makes the coffee more acidic.

like peppermint, pumpkin pie, gingerbread or cinnamon, topped with whipped cream and sprinkles. Liquid Christmas.

"A gingerbread latte?"

My mom nodded. "Make that two."

We picked up our drinks and settled in at a tiny table. We were both a little out of our coffee comfort zone; my mom never had something that sweet and in a paper cup to boot, and me, well, it was coffee.

I took a cautious sip.

My mom took a cautious sip.

And then something surprising happened.

"This is good," my mom declared.

"It is good!"

The next year during the Christmas holidays, we found ourselves in the same coffee shop. And the year after that. It's a new rule, you see. Mothers and daughters must drink gingerbread lattes together at least once during the holidays. No exceptions allowed.

Michelle Mach

Salute! LeChaim! Bonzai! To Life!

Don't criticize my coffee.
Some day you, too, may be old and weak.

Author Unknown

arl loves coffee. When he walks into a room, his essence is of a robust Colombian. We met almost twenty years ago at a tai chi class, and we've been friends ever since. He sips coffee longingly, like a baby sips his bottle. Caffeine does not affect his personality or his demeanor; he is well-balanced and grounded, no pun intended, with almost a laissez-faire attitude. He smiles constantly, but saves his seriousness for the big battles that need to be fought.

Earl visits a local coffee shop almost daily, discussing current events and philosophy with friends and colleagues. Earl knows I'm also a coffee aficionado, and when the mood strikes, he invites me to hang out just to talk. I knew something was up when he called one day; his voice wasn't his normal, happy tone. There was a hint of concern as he spoke.

Earl was recently diagnosed with prostate cancer and underwent radiation therapy. I'm a cancer survivor myself. Earl has prostate; I have ovarian. He and I talk about our cancer strategies. We plan and map out how to win life and combat cancer. We brace each other up with a pure desire for living. Our chemotherapies are discussed over our yin/yang of coffees; mine—black his—light cream with lots of sugar. We both have the attitude that we will be victorious. Earl says he wants to live another fifteen years; it would make him ninety-four. I always tell him he'll be a centenarian, and I will help him blow out his 100 candles as I become an octogenarian. But we both know that it's one day at a time that gets us through. We joke about how coffee could kill us, and then laugh, remembering that if cancer hasn't, why worry?

Earl and I leave the coffee house in peaceful, yet uplifted spirits, knowing all is right with our world. We know we can't prevent wars, stop starvation, and annihilate plagues all by ourselves, but we can set our intentions for the process to begin as our thoughts are real things that affect the universe. And, most of all, we know it begins by first fixing ourselves. In the meantime, we can send goodwill and much love to the universe.

I raise my mug to Earl. To life—and to many more lessons for a long, long time to come, over a nice, steamy cup of hot coffee.

Dolores Kozielski

No Two Cups Alike

In most households, a cup of coffee
is considered the one thing
needful at the breakfast hour.

Janet McKenzie Hill

Jerry and I have known each other for forty years. We share living quarters and enjoy our time together, but we both like freedom—to pursue our individual quests. Our separate grown children don't need us much, since they're all wonderfully independent. Though retired, we tend to spend work hours apart and link up for meals here and there, or in the coffee shops around town.

Jerry and I both love coffee. We each have a favorite cup: his from his other life with his wife of thirty years, and mine from my former life with my husband of twenty-two years. Jerry's cup is small, made of white porcelain, a sort of refined mug, pentagonal in shape. My mug is shorter and wider, with wavy brown, rust, and white vertical stripes—stoneware really. These cups look like us. Jerry is more proper and traditional than me. I am more rustic and casual than him. Jerry's cup has chips in the rim and the base. Mine is run through with multiple mini-cracks that look like a maze of tiny roads on a city map, but no chips.

Recently, a friend told me I should "disappear" Jerry's cup to save him from lead poisoning where the glaze is worn off. But he's so attached to it I'm not sure what the consequences would be—even the unspoken ones. Better the poison. Our cabinets are filled with matching cups, but if our favorite, old-time cups are available—that is, if they are clean and on the shelf—we go for them.

Now why do we hang on to these last vestiges of our former lives? I can only reason that the cups represent the years and not the former spouses. Jerry's wife had fits of temper—tossed his clothes out the window, locked him out of the house, and changed the locks on the doors, for example. My husband usually spent our wedding anniversaries in another country, celebrating his mother's birthday, for another example.

In fact, when Jerry and I found each other again, we admired a teddy bear in a store covered in calico patches. We bought the wounded bear. "That's us," we said. And ever since, the teddy bear is a symbol of our affection for each other. I got the coffee habit during nurse's training in the late fifties and early sixties, the years when I first knew Jerry, who interned at Grady Hospital in Atlanta, and trained for doctoring while I trained for nursing at another hospital.

My roommates and I drank coffee from short, wide water glasses to stay awake to study, until the brew, once nasty to the tongue, began to taste good. None of us possessed a coffee mug—most of us were poor, otherwise we would have attended a proper college somewhere—and the hospital didn't provide them, so after the coffee was poured, you had to wait until it cooled down before you could hold onto the glass tumbler. I still have an image of that aromatic coffee, generously laced with full milk, wafting its curls of steam, waiting to be drunk. Those water glasses without handles are the other "coffee cups" I remember affectionately.

Inexplicably, about a week ago and during the time I've been writing this piece, as I unloaded the dishwasher my thirty-three-year-old favorite mug fell from my fingers to the stone floor in the kitchen and smashed into pieces. Is this a sign? Will I shop for another one? That pattern of stoneware is still available. I saw it not too many years ago in Dillard's. But no, maybe Jerry's cup will break soon, and I'll go out and buy a pair of glass cups—with handles—put them on the kitchen shelf, and see what happens.

Ellen Hunter Ulken

How Much Is Enough?

The taste of coffee is an individual thing. How much to use is one of the many decisions you will be faced with when brewing a pot.

If you know your bean, the guessing is less, but if you are trying something new, the freshness of the bean, the variety of coffee, the size of the grind, and the brewing method you choose will all make a difference in how much you use.

In general, though, the Specialty Coffee Association of America (SCAA) offers this advice. A standard cup of coffee is considered to be six ounces. For each six ounces, use 1–2 tablespoons of freshly ground coffee. If you don't grind your own, the coffee is likely to be less flavorful, but increasing the proportion will only result in a stronger, more acidic taste, not a more flavorful brew.

Arigato!

The tempo, the complexity, the tension
of modern life call for something
that can perform the miracle of
stimulating brain activity.

Margaret Meagher

Entering a Starbucks in Kanazawa, Japan, gave me quite a jolt. Emotional, that is. The coffee house looked so different from any I'd been to in the States. But why did my husband and I need a Starbucks, anyway? Here we were, in this exotic castle town untouched by World War II.

We needed coffee, that's why. After days of nonstop drizzle, our umbrellas had become extensions of our bodies. Overseas Adventure Travel had been running our small group joyously ragged with its exhilarating, high-intensity days led by Ms. Junko Ito, an expert local guide.

On our first morning in Kanazawa, we trekked along the cobblestoned streets of the historic Nagamachi quarter, filled with samurais' homes. I got the shivers when I saw the latticework windows. Behind them, the samurais' guards would sit, their swords at the ready, peering out unseen, but able to scrutinize all who passed by or approached the door.

Next, we visited Kenroku-en, one of the three most fabulous gardens in all of Japan. We strolled among the 12,000 trees, over charming bridges, and beside serene ponds tended by local gardeners. Their reflections appeared in the mirrored waters as they gently weeded and pruned shrubs and branches.

My feet started dragging. My legs weighed a hundred pounds apiece. Had we walked two miles, or twelve? At an exquisite teahouse inside the gardens, we were graced with a solemn, traditional tea ceremony. The tiny pastries tasted delicious, pampering my palate like marzipan, my favorite sweet. But the green tea met my tongue with a thick and slightly weird texture. Where was my coffee? Not here, of course. Oh, boy. How was I going to negotiate another eight hours of shrines, handicraft centers, and markets? Not to mention Buddhist temples: shoes off, shoes on, shoes off, shoes on.

Junko, always sympathetic and sensitive to our needs, announced an afternoon break to do whatever we wished. Like homing pigeons, Larry and I headed to the Starbucks near our hotel, in the Musashimachi shopping complex. What was it that startled me as I set foot inside? Every coffee shop I've ever visited in the United States has signaled one message—this is a utilitarian, commercial establishment where you pay for your order, stay for a bit, and leave to make room for other customers. Not this Starbucks.

It was so uncommercial! It consisted of two rooms. The first one was like entering a comfy living room, crowded with sofas and puffy armchairs. The place seemed to be geared to students, who sat in heavy silence as they pored over notebooks, textbooks or perhaps novels. No one looked up when we entered. Everyone seemed totally focused on their work. They looked as if they'd been there for hours and planned to stay for at least a few more. The upholstery almost appeared to be growing around them. Everyone sipped or munched. Some of the cups and plates were empty, yet no manager hovered over a shoulder, hinting that it was time to order something more or leave.

The second, much larger room—the main area of the café—contained no couches or easy chairs. There was the counter for ordering, of course, and typical small, round tables. But in the center was a long polished-wood table with two lamps on it: brass lamps with green plastic shades. A study table! How incredibly thoughtful of management. A girl hunched over her notebook, vigorously writing math problems. Across the table, a young man with highlighter in hand flipped through pages of a large tome.

Savor the Flavor

Arabicas boast a wide range of flavors. Before roasting, the smell of a handful of Arabica beans smells of blueberries. That fruity quality translates well after roasting and results in a sweet smell to the roasted beans. Seventy percent of the world's coffee production is the Arabica species.

Robustas tend to produce a nutty, grainy smell before roasting, like peanuts or oats. Most often, a roasted robusta bean will smell burnt, even when roasted properly. Some say the smell is akin to burnt rubber or plastic.

Curiously, in the entire café, we saw not one laptop computer. Maybe they're too expensive for young people in Japan. Or maybe too clumsy to carry about.

I got so wrapped up in this remarkable scene that I almost forgot what I'd come for—a decadent white-chocolate mocha. My virtuous husband ordered decaf coffee. The tables were so small that Larry and I played "kneesy" and "footsy" as we savored our drinks. We lingered long after we'd finished, basking in the local atmosphere.

Culturally, the Japanese place a high priority on their children's education. That value was clearly demonstrated by this particular coffee house in its underlying kindness toward the young students. In this day of bottom lines and balance sheets, I found their approach both touching and refreshing. For this I say, *Arigato!* Thank you!

Rosemary Mild

Why Is It That... Coffee Is Legal? (But I'm Sure Glad It Is!)

Given enough coffee, I could rule the world.

Author Unknown

Whenever I reach a state of caffeinated nirvana, I stop to ponder how something that makes me instantly soothed and perky can possibly be legal. The mere idea that the Surgeon General could order those magical beans off the shelves and out of my life has me scheming toward the type of stock-up that even Costco couldn't supply. My fear is that these thoughts alone make me something of a textbook junkie. This is particularly clear when I confess to fantasizing about my next fix before the one I'm savoring has neither been finished nor gone cold. But before you go coordinating an intervention, please concede that there are benefits to spending time with a grown woman who indulges in such a deliciously harmless vice.

My husband sees the advantages so clearly that I'm afraid I might soon awaken with the tubes of a House Blend IV lodged in my arm as he tries to speed up my morning metamorphosis. For now, without the benefit of

a slow drip of drip to jump-start my day, he's stuck with a
grumbling and disheveled woman who stumbles out of
bed at the insistence of two annoyingly playful cubs.
Before my eyes can even focus, our girls are ready to don
their jazz pants and dance to the Pure Disco CD. At this
hour, the music of my youth sounds much more like white
noise. The actress in me does her very best to be
impressed by their lead-footed jetés as I gulp down that
first cup of the day.

Within minutes . . . yeah! Mom is back in action. I'm
ready to fix breakfast, pack lunches and, after a rare good
night's sleep and an especially dark brew, even bust a few
dance moves with the girls. I refer to this, the euphoric
time period after my first cup, as "BC" (Blissfully
Caffeinated). It is when the cobwebs clear and the feeling
of hope returns to my normally happy and optimistic
persona.

This, my friends, is the most enjoyable yet dangerous
time of day. You see, the day is new, and the caffeine is
pumping through and putting the spice back in this Spice
Girl. Oh, the things I am going to accomplish today!

I know my addiction is worsening since the same high I
used to get from one cup is now coming from two.
Between you and me, when I'm in a real pinch of afternoon lethargy, I sometimes even push the envelope with
a third cup. I do this well aware of the risk I run of sending myself into a Tasmanian Devil-like frenzy that will
leave anyone within a three-house radius wishing they
had a basement to shield them from the fallout. I'm smart
enough to realize that the physical rush that coffee brings

me is too good to be healthy, but I'm hooked enough to do nothing about it. I'm comforted and validated by the solidarity I share with the nine or more similarly addicted individuals who wait in line like me for their sixteen ounces of wake-up.

My only fear, as I tap my foot impatiently while awaiting my turn, is that one of the employees will single me out by calling me "Norm" and slide my usual order to the end of the bar. Only then will I concede that I've gone too far and will sadly slink to step two in the recovery process. But until I find myself with a reserved seat next to an all-knowing mail carrier at the coffee bar, or that dastardly Surgeon General deems my consumption illegal, I will continue to caffeinate.

My reasoning is part selfish pleasure and part public service. Because the way I see it, at least eighty-four people, including my family, friends, and the unsuspecting strangers whom I wave to with all five fingers as I let them merge onto the freeway, are counting on me to be full of life and energy. And with only a three-dollar investment, I won't soon be letting them down.

Shana McLean Moore

Ice Is Nice

> The discovery of coffee has enlarged
> the realm of illusion and given
> more promise to hope.
>
> *Isidore Bourdon*

D rinking iced coffee in the summer is a pleasure.
Drinking iced coffee all year 'round—especially
when the weather turns cold—is an act of devo-
tion, a commitment.

"Are you sure you want that with ice, honey?" the
woman behind the counter at my favorite independent
coffee shop asks, shaking her head. "It's awfully cold out
there today." I know she means well, so I smile, thank her
for her concern, and repeat my order. Firmly. "One iced
mocha, please."

This exchange has become routine for me. Although I
order iced coffee, iced lattes, iced mochaccinos, and all
manner of iced concoctions throughout the torrid summer
months, I also drink them in the fall, the spring, and on the
bitterest winter days. There's just something about iced
mochas that is simultaneously decadent and innocent—
sipping what looks and feels like a milkshake when it's
barely 8:00 AM. You can't sip a steaming-hot pumpkin latte

through a straw, or you'll get bits of melted plastic in your drink. Iced drinks are beautifully portable, difficult to spill, never burning your fingers. And the ice seems to enhance the sweetness of chocolate and other flavors. Even spectacularly strong, bitter coffee can make for a good iced coffee drink if it is properly made.

But in the first nippy chill of autumn, there's a sea change at the coffee shop. Even though the calendar still says it's officially summer, the signs indicate that fall is very much on the way. Nubby sweaters wave from department-store window displays. Children gaze despairingly at school supplies now lining the shelves at the local big-box store. And, incomprehensibly to me, some stores take iced coffee off their menus. Happily, I'm not alone in my obsession for iced coffee year-round. Apparently it's an international phenomenon.

On a recent trip to Japan, I was delighted to find that even the smallest coffee counters sold iced lattes, and the ubiquitous vending machines dispensed miniature cans of super-sweet Coffee Boss and other brands of coffee drinks, often with milk and sugar already added into the can.

A friend living in Italy swears by the Shakerato technique—using a martini shaker to tumble a double shot of espresso and ice, then straining only the chilled drink into a glass. And Vietnamese-style iced coffee, made sweet and strong with condensed milk and a coffee-and-chicory blend, is another way to get a fix.

It seems like everyone has their own tricks for creating the perfect iced-coffee concoction. I know one person who swears by coffee frozen into ice cubes so that it won't dilute the ideal milk-to-coffee ratio when the ice cubes melt. Another insists that two heaping teaspoons of instant espresso powder added to extra-strong coffee makes for the best brew. And yet a third recommends using coffee-flavored syrup to create a smooth, sweet iced drink.

Perhaps the reason iced-coffee fanatics are so particular is that unlike hot coffee, which can mask all kinds of deficiencies beneath its enticing aroma, cold coffee shows off the range of coffee flavors—including the bitter and the refrigerated-stale.

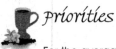 *Priorities*

For the average coffee drinker, freshly ground beans, clean equipment, and good quality water are generally more important than the quality of your beans or how long it's been since they were roasted.

I have my own requirements for my daily iced mocha: it should be made with chocolate syrup, not grainy powdered chocolate, and the order in which the ingredients are combined is critical. Pour cold milk over ice cubes in a glass. In a separate cup, combine hot, fresh espresso and chocolate syrup, and then stir that into the milk and ice. If the hot espresso is poured over plain ice cubes, you wind up with watery espresso and no ice. If the chocolate is poured in too late, after the drink is chilled, it clumps and doesn't blend in.

I raise my glass of iced mocha, ice cubes clinking together, straw at the perfect forty-five-degree angle for sipping, and admire the drink inside—a rainbow of rich browns, lighter at the top, drawing darker with sunken chocolate at the bottom. This is a perfect summer drink, yes, but also refreshing in the winter, spring, and yes, autumn.

"Your usual?" asks the woman behind the counter at the local coffee shop, just a few days after she shook her head in disbelief at my cold-weather, iced-mocha order. She calls over to the young man with the goatee at the end of the counter: "One skim mo, to go!" These are sweet words to hear indeed.

Kara Newman

"Better bring the pot back over here, Mom,
Dad's still down a couple of cups."

Fragrant Memories

Coffee, according to the women of
Denmark, is to the body what the
Word of the Lord is to the soul.

Isak Dinesen

F or most people, coffee is all about the taste. Preferences range from light, mellow and subtle, to full-bodied, distinctive and vibrant. Not for me. For me, it's all about the aroma. In fact, the moment the rich aroma of roasted coffee beans permeates the air, or the heady scent of brewing coffee fills the room . . .

I'm six years old again, peering into the formal dining room as aunts, uncles, parents, and grandparents linger over Sunday dinner. Plates piled high with Italian pastries are passed as the grown-ups drink fresh-brewed coffee from fragile, gold-rimmed china cups decorated with hand-painted flowers.

I'm thirteen years old, having my first sip of coffee from a yellow Tupperware mug with my mother and a neighbor. More milk than coffee, nevertheless it's a privilege to be included at the table with the adults.

I'm sixteen, drinking a cup of instant coffee—not just a

sip or two—with friends, unsure of myself, but eager to prove I fit in.

I'm eighteen, celebrating high-school graduation at an elegant restaurant with my family. Complementing the elaborate dessert is a steaming cup of coffee—a very "adult" way to end this significant day.

I'm nineteen, consuming gallons of caffeinated coffee, frantically trying to survive late-night study sessions and early-morning college classes.

I'm twenty, sharing wedding cake and coffee with 130 of our closest friends and family. Surrounded by the glow of their good wishes, I bask in the dream of a happy-ever-after with the man of my dreams.

I'm thirty, grabbing a Styrofoam cup from the coffee cart at the office, part of the team, climbing the rungs of management, excited about advancing my career.

I'm forty-eight, meeting friends at a coffee house, struggling to decipher the difference between a latte and a cappuccino. The air is infused with aromatic promise and the joy of anticipation. Life is good.

Rich, steaming, slow-roasted, fresh-brewed coffee—I can smell the memories!

Ava Pennington

An Intergenerational Love Affair

The best maxim I know in this life is to drink
your coffee when you can, and when you
cannot, to be easy without it.

Jonathan Swift

I t was the late 1940s, and I huddled in my grandmother's kitchen on a chilly summer morning in
northern Minnesota. Waves of heat rippled from
the wood-burning kitchen stove. The gray granite coffee
boiler bubbled merrily. My grandmother, with her
chipped coffee cup never far from her hands, fried bacon
and eggs in a blur of delicious farmhouse smells. Carl, my
step-grandfather, stomped into the kitchen after milking
the cows. The odor of warm hay and fresh dew evaporated
from his clothes as he bent over the sink to wash his
hands, and splash his face and the back of his neck.

I once read, "Nothing is more memorable than smell."
As an adult, I retrieve that special memory of my grandparents as I relax by the fire reading the *New York Times* on
a blistery Sunday morning with a steaming mug of coffee.
But it's more than a memory—it's the feelings and emotions I hold for two very special people.

I remember the warmth. I think of my grandmother

now, in one of her flowered housedresses that my mom sewed each summer when we visited, her white hair pulled back in a bun, sitting at the table with a hot cup of coffee. She'd smile at the friend who'd stopped by to visit. Placing her hands on the table, she'd give a push, and slowly rise. "Let me get you a cup of coffee."

A weekly event during my summer visit was a trip to town for my grandmother's doctor's appointment. My special treat was selecting a cup and saucer at the pharmacy before trudging upstairs for an update on her heart-related problems and asthma. This collection is now in my buffet. The ebony set with gold trim was my favorite, but my daughters had their own favorites. They arranged the sets on the dining-room table and presided over coffee parties with their dolls. These cups will be my legacy to them one day.

As a child in Silver Spring, Maryland, a hot breakfast was also a part of our routine, but it wasn't the same. The wood-burning stove and my grandparents were missing. I hid my scrambled eggs under a napkin, and rushed off to the bus stop as soon as I could escape to grab extra minutes with friends. My dad was in a hurry, too . . . listening for the beep of the horn from a carpooling friend. He'd pour his coffee into his saucer to cool. Then picking the saucer up with both hands, he'd sip the coffee, quite properly with his thick pinky fingers protruding upward.

"My dad always said," he'd comment, "it's okay to drink coffee from a saucer as long as you raise your pinky." Such was my lesson in the etiquette of coffee-saucer slurping.

But now I drink coffee in mugs. The habit of cups and

saucers are another world, another era. I sit with my coffee, warming my hands around a mug, leaning forward in care to a good friend's outpouring of hurt and anger. I reach for the empty mug and refill it. I remember other moments, when another friend nourishes my broken hopes. We sit at her kitchen table, mugs in hand, staring at the woods behind her house. New seeds are planted. A cardinal lifts her wings . . . she lifts her mug in a toast to me.

I've now gathered my grandchildren into the coffee fold. They've learned to brew coffee. When once they stood on chairs, they now plant their feet on the floor. When once I steadied their hands as they scooped the coffee beans into the grinder, they now do so themselves. As two-year-olds, I held them in my arms, with their hands over their ears as I pressed the coffee-grinder lever. But life flits forward. After a sleepover with my nine-year-old grandson, Jack, I walk down the stairs to the smell of coffee. He hands me a mug of coffee he has prepared. We sit down to talk. It's a new generation of coffee memories.

Elizabeth H. Phillips-Hershey, Ph.D.

Not Such a Bitter Brew

At low levels, the ever-present bitterness of coffee adds a flavor dimension and helps counteract acidity. The roast, the mineral content of the water, the water temperature, the brewing time, grind size, and brewing method all affect the bitterness of your coffee.

Medium roasts have less soluble solids, a higher acid content, and a more potent aroma . . . all things that reduce perceived bitterness.

Filtered water is preferred for brewing good coffee. Filtering improves the taste and odor of water and removes some contaminants.

Add a pinch of sodium chloride (salt), sucrose (sugar or vanilla extract) or citric acid (orange peel) to your ground coffee before brewing to reduce the perception of bitterness. Some folks swear by rinsed eggshells.

Coffee soaked in fresh water for twenty-four hours after fermentation—a process known as wet-processing and popular with producers in Kenya—is less bitter than dry processed coffee.

Drip brewers produce fewer soluble solids and result in a less bitter brew as compared to other brewing methods.

The finer the grind, the more bitter the flavor. It's important to match the grind size to the brewing method, so if your brew is bitter, don't adjust the grind—try another brewing method.

The Truth About Coffee

Chocolate, men, coffee—
some things are better rich.

Author Unknown

"Thanks, Trisha. Dinner was grrreat," my husband purred to our sister-in-law. Mike and I had driven down from Milwaukee to spend a couple of days at my brother Jim's in Illinois.

Now it was time for our customary river-walk through their beautiful town of Naperville. It was one of those perfect winter evenings when only a light jacket and scarf were needed. The air was fresh, and a soft snowfall kept our path bright as we followed the flow of the river for nearly an hour.

"We'd better head back," Jim cautioned. "We don't want you old fogies making any excuses about being too tired to win at Scrabble." And so we turned toward home to pursue our traditional family word-game challenges.

Arriving home, we all instinctively made our way to the fireplace in the den. Now it was my turn to purr. "Oh, this is sooo nice and cozy. Maybe I am too tired for games."

"I'm pretty tired, too," Mike agreed.

"I hate to admit it, but me, too," Jim confessed. "Guess that walk did us all in."

"Well," Trisha suggested, "how about I put on a pot of coffee to wake us up?"

"That'll work," we all agreed as we made our way to the kitchen table.

"Remember when we were in college cramming for exams and gulping down coffee all night to stay awake?" Mike asked.

"Yes," we all chimed.

"And during the teachers' strike when we were on the picket line and it was freezing cold," I reminisced, "that hot coffee got us through some pretty hard days."

"Remember when Dad was in the hospital after his heart attack?" Jim reminded. "The hours we spent in the lounge sipping coffee and comforting each other? It was like the best drug in the world."

"And how many times did we stay up most of the night talking and drinking coffee on Christmas Eve after we got all the kids in bed?" Trisha asked.

"Well, let's hope it works tonight, because I really want to beat you youngsters in Password!" I spouted.

Trisha poured the coffee, and as we inhaled the rich aroma there was an almost unanimous "Mmmm" from around the table. After a few sips, we all began to come to life. "This is working!" Mike said. "I feel better already."

"Me, too," I agreed.

"Yep," Jim said, "let the games begin!"

We were enjoying our time together. And it seemed the more coffee we drank, the more we came alive with laughter. We paused after the second game so Trisha could make a fresh pot.

"This java has done the trick once again," I exclaimed, holding up my mug.

"You're right. The caffeine is working," Jim agreed.

"I feel wide awake now," Mike said.

In the next instant, we heard Trisha giggling in the pantry. It was a contagious sound that tickled us. "Trisha, what's so funny?" we called to her. She stepped back into the kitchen. With her shoulders still shaking from laughter, she held up the can of coffee and pointed to the lettering: DECAFFEINATED. "Honest," she said, "I didn't know."

After some really good belly laughs, we realized that the power of suggestion is a mighty force. And in the end, we decided it really wasn't the caffeine that kept us going throughout the years when we needed a lift. It was the camaraderie—the closeness of family and friends that pulled us through those times. But we all agreed that it wouldn't have been the same without those tasty sips of coffee to warm us up, to stimulate conversation, and to give us something to hold onto for enjoyment or for comfort. Like a good friend, it was always there when needed— sometimes with caffeine; sometimes without!

Kay Conner Pliszka

Touched by a Coffee-Loving Angel

Behind every successful woman is a
substantial amount of coffee.

Stephanie Piro

here were no customers in line at the Java Hut
when I dashed up to the counter with my arms
waving and shouting, "I need a cup of hazelnut
coffee to go, please!" The woman behind the register was a
stranger to me, someone new, who obviously wasn't
accustomed to my frantic outbursts. With hands on her
hips, she countered, "Do you always demand your coffee
that way?"

Embarrassed, I offered, "No, not always, but I'm late for
work, and I can't live without my hazelnut coffee!"
Quickly eyeing her name badge, I added, "Thank you,
Linda."

While she poured my coffee, I couldn't help but notice
the gorgeous, long-stemmed pink roses in a crystal vase
sitting on the counter.

"Is it your birthday?" I asked.

She turned around and whispered, "No, it's mammogram day!" She saw the puzzled look on my face and
leaned in closer. "I'm always nervous on the day of my

mammogram, so my husband sends me flowers. I've had a few close calls, so it gets harder every year."

"How thoughtful of your husband. What a gem."

Linda reached out her hand with my cup of coffee, while I blurted out, "I've never had a mammogram, and my mom was diagnosed with breast cancer five years ago."

Suddenly, Linda glared at me and snapped, "You're not getting this until you get a mammogram, and that's final!"

I was shocked. I thought she was joking until I saw the steam rising, and it wasn't from the coffee. Linda refused to serve me, and I left vowing never to return. I drove to work coffee-less and miserable with a pounding headache. The entire day, I couldn't shake the java outburst. While driving home, and later that evening on the treadmill at the gym, Linda's words haunted me. I was forty years old and in the best shape of my life, but I knew it was foolish to take a family history of breast cancer lightly.

That night after I showered, no doubt because my encounter with Linda was still fresh on my mind, I performed a rare breast self-examination. My hand froze. No, it can't be, I thought, as my fingers paused over the coffee-bean-sized lump. Panicked, I pounced on the bed where my husband of twenty years was snoring peacefully, "Wake up, honey, please. I found a lump. I think I have breast cancer."

Mark, nearly immune to my hypochondriac tendencies and only semi-conscious, was not amused. "Sure you do, sweetheart. Now go back to sleep." I was horrified. I tried to explain the day's events: Linda at the Java Hut, the coffee that I didn't receive, the mammogram I should have scheduled, and now the lump. Out of pure exhaustion, I drifted off to sleep, only to wake up with a note pasted to my left cheek. I had rolled over on it sometime in the early morning. It read, "I went running. Coffee is brewing. Call the doctor. Love, Mark!"

I padded downstairs in my pink bunny slippers and called our family physician. He reassured me that I was overreacting but, just in case, he ordered a mammogram for that Monday.

The day of my mammogram, Mark met me at the clinic. When my name was called, I almost ran back to the parking lot. Instead, I dutifully followed the young technician. The smell of coffee in the nurse's lounge wafted through the air and put me at ease. This wasn't going to be so bad. But the look on the technician's face told a different story. She tried to hide her concern, but I could feel her become more tense each time she came in with the radiologist's order for another view. Finally, she pronounced, "The radiologist wants you to have a sonogram." As I lay there in the dark, I realized this was serious. The technician said, "You can get dressed; the radiologist would like to speak with you."

On March 21, 1996, I heard the words, "You have breast cancer." I was in shock as I struggled through surgery, treatment, and finally radiation. But through it all, I couldn't shake the feeling that Linda at the Java Hut had saved my life. Had I not gone for coffee that day and Linda been there to (not) serve me, who knows what would have happened.

Three months after my surgery, I returned to thank Linda. I waited in line until the last customer was served and then asked, "Do you remember me?" Linda hesitated slightly and said, "Oh, yes! Did you get your mammogram?"

I fought back tears as I spoke. "Yes, I did. In fact, I think you saved my life!" Linda looked puzzled. I explained the events that had transpired since that fateful day in March. Linda listened intently, and then tears formed in her eyes. I reached in my purse and handed her an angel pin that a friend gave me right before my surgery. I had worn it every day since, and now it was my turn to pass it on. I reached over the granite counter and pinned it on Linda's pink and white collar. She touched its wings and said, "I'm so thankful you're doing so well. Oh, and by the way, I owe you a cup of coffee. You won't believe what our special is today—Frangelica Hazelnut Coffee."

There we stood in the Java Hut with our paper cups filled with coffee, toasting to my new life. Linda smiled and asked, "So how is it?"

I grinned, savoring the aroma and reveling in the flavor of life. "Angelic. It's absolutely angelic."

Connie K. Pombo

Mom's Coffeepot

Mothers are those wonderful people
who can get up in the morning
before the smell of coffee.

Author Unknown

y mother just loved coffee. She drank it from early morning until late at night, and still could get a solid night's sleep. It wasn't that she was immune to the caffeine. It was because she had shared her coffee that day with every neighbor, transient, family member, and new friend until she dropped into bed, tired but content. Our sink was never cleared of dishes. As fast as they were washed, it soon held more. Only at the end of the day did anyone see our gleaming white sink cleared and clean of lovingly used cups and plates.

Early in her married life, Mom got used to drinking her coffee strong. From necessity, it became a habit. She'd put on a fresh pot, the phone would ring, and she'd soon be in deep conversation with someone needing a ride to the doctor, help with an unpaid bill, or just wanting someone sympathetic to talk to at that moment. While she was on the phone, the coffee would perk and perk, sometimes for twenty minutes or more. Thinking it was ready, we'd turn it off before her conversation ended. She'd hang up the phone, come into our kitchen, and say, "Who turned off the coffee? It has to perk just a little more." Then she'd turn on the burner again until the beverage was thick and nourishing.

Her coffee was sustenance to many, and its warming aroma filled our home all day long. It wasn't until I was grown and a busy mother of four myself that I realized how Mom thrived by drinking that delicious coffee. I finally understood how coffee kept her going every day. No matter how busy she was, when someone in need knocked, she'd hustle over to the door, invite that person in, and sit them down with a cup of her welcoming aromatic brew, a donut or toast and jelly, and oftentimes a complete meal, which she could whip up in what seemed like minutes.

As they explained their urgent situation, I'd hear her say to them, "Now you just relax and enjoy your food and coffee, and we'll get this problem figured out." Somehow, she always managed to do exactly that. It seemed there was never a problem my mother couldn't conquer. At her kitchen table, new laws were formatted to protect the elderly. She'd present them to City Hall, and they would often pass. Shaky marriages were put back together. Plans were made to get a sick animal to the vet. Over her cup of brew, she signed military papers and sent them to the Army. Their purpose? Our widowed neighbor across the street was very ill and lived alone. Those papers convinced the Army to discharge her son from the service to take care of his mother; he was home in a matter of weeks.

My mom has passed away now, but she's still very close in my heart. Every time I smell coffee brewing in my own kitchen, I remember her coffeepot perking away and see her hustling around, administering to everyone's needs but her own. To my mother, a steaming-hot cup of coffee was more than just something to drink. It was her way of providing warm, loving comfort to others.

Kay Presto

Life Cycle of a Mother's Cup of Coffee

Honeymoon: Hubby leaves a steaming mug of java on bedside table as your wake-up alarm.

Pregnancy: The smell of coffee brewing spins you on your heels to run to the nearest bathroom.

Newborn: Coffee and nursing incompatible; fight sleep by sniffing coffee beans.

Infancy: Fresh pot of hot water. Forgot to put the coffee in the filter or forgot to plug it in.

Crawler: No milk? No problem. Squirt formula from bottle into coffee cup.

Toddler: Several cups of coffee strategically located in high places around the house.

School years: Contemplate installing a mini-coffeemaker in the car as you're endlessly chauffeuring. Starbucks cups litter the van floor. They belong to your kids. You don't have time (or money) to go to Starbucks.

College years: Coffee maker keeps disappearing and resurfacing in dorm rooms. You have bought as many new coffee makers as you have children.

Empty nester: You have finished your first cup of coffee, while it is still hot, in almost twenty years.

Golden years: Hubby leaves a steaming mug of java on your bedside table. You both go back to sleep.

Christa Allan

3

RELAXING RENDEZVOUS

The Best Part of Waking Up

No coffee can be good in the mouth
that does not first send a sweet offering
of odor to the nostrils.

Henry Ward Beecher

I 've never been a coffee drinker—unless, of course, you count the sip I sneaked at age five. Recently deemed old enough to pour and carry an insulated mug of his favorite brew to Daddy, I hesitated in the kitchen. Recalling his detailed instructions, I stirred in a heaping teaspoon of sugar followed by a swirl of thick cream. And I knew the exact measurement of a swirl because I'd watched him do it countless times. Add a splash of cream before twirling the mug between his work-rough palms and inhaling. He made it look so, so desirable. Yet . . . "Coffee isn't for little girls," he'd say when I begged for a drink. "It'll put hair on your chest."

Steadying the steaming coffee between both chubby hands, I inched my way from the room, careful not to slosh. Tendrils of fragrant Folgers teased my nose. Tempted by the milky-sweet scent, I actually did it—I took a quick sip.

Today, I recall the scald more than the taste—which was

surely overshadowed by my blistered tongue.

Even so, I still can't resist the smell of coffee. To me, it's redolent of home; it spells D-a-d-d-y.

Mother rose early on weekdays solely to have the pot percolated by the time Dad had dressed and shaved for work. I woke to the peppy sound and scent every morning of my childhood. In later years, my gadget-minded father purchased the first timed coffee brewer to hit the market. After that, they took turns setting it to perk so that they, too, awoke to the scent.

On our annual summer camping trips to the Rocky Mountains, Daddy was the early riser. In the crisp predawn, he flexed his arms and chopped wood, setting aside the splinters for kindling. Before long, a fire flamed in the rock-ringed pit while a sooty coffeepot bubbled on its fringes. In a huge iron skillet, he fried bacon to a crisp and reserved the grease for a mess of hash browns. As he cracked eggs into the pan, he called us from the tent.

"Coffee's on!" he whisper-shouted, to avoid disturbing other campers. He never announced breakfast itself, the filling meal-for-six he'd lovingly prepared for us all. A simple "Coffee's on!" said it all.

The first time I brought home my husband-to-be, Daddy took him aside for a manly visit over a cup of coffee. It was a privilege I'd never been afforded. And, from across the kitchen, Daddy looked at me, raised an eyebrow . . . and winked his approval.

My daddy died a few years back. When I went back to visit Mother sometime later, his absence in the house was heart-wrenching. One morning, I spoke up.

"Everything feels different without Daddy. It even smells different."

I stared down into my glass of orange juice and frowned. "That's it!" I looked at Mother. "The smell of coffee! Why don't I smell coffee?"

She shook her head with a sad smile. "No need to brew a pot with only me here to drink it. I just heat a cupful at a time in the microwave."

A sad state of affairs, for certain. But, of course, she was right. Still, the house no longer smelled like home.

Maybe that's why I burn coffee-scented candles in my own house. Why I sniff appreciatively in out-of-the-way diners. Why I sometimes accept a brimming cupful to roll between my palms. It affords me opportunities to inhale the memories.

Still, I can't quite bring myself to drink the stuff. I don't want to worry about getting hair on my chest!

Carol McAdoo Rehme

coffee cupping

Cupping is an essential process in detecting defective coffee and in creating blends. It is a tasting technique used to evaluate the aroma and flavor profile of a coffee. The profile consists of:

Fragrance: the smell of ground coffee before the addition of water.

Aroma: the smell when coffee is first exposed to the wet grounds.

Flavor: a term that encompasses all the other coffee-cupping parameters.

Acidity: akin to the sensation when drinking a red wine; it's the bright and dry taste experienced on the backside of your tongue.

A Lesson in Forgiveness

The love of our neighbor in all its fullness
simply means being able to say to him,
"What are you going through?"

Simone Weil

It was snowing as I finished unbuckling my baby from her car seat. A toot from behind reminded me that I was holding up traffic on the one-way street.

I didn't care. My six-month-old had to get an immunization, which meant she would be up all night with a fever. My head ached like I was coming down with the flu, and my husband's job didn't look steady for the holidays. I wasn't in a good mood.

The truck tooted its horn again. When I finally had my little one in my arms and covered from the cold air, I looked up and felt my heart sink. I had inadvertently parked in a delivery zone. A look at the name printed on the truck confirmed that I was parked in its delivery zone.

Angry at myself for not noticing the sign sooner, I put my baby back into the car and looked down the street. The nearest empty place was more than a block away. Gritting my teeth, I was tempted to go home and reschedule my baby's vaccination for a day when things were going better, but I didn't.

After managing to parallel park in a tight spot, I again got ready to get out of my car. Glancing up, I saw someone waiting for me outside. I knew it was the truck driver. Bracing myself for a verbal attack, I slowly emerged from the car.

"Sorry about that back there." A strong note of apology rang in the man's voice. I looked at him suspiciously. He was actually grinning at me!

"I saw you had a baby," he continued, "but there wasn't any other place big enough for me to park in."

I managed to stammer my own apology, though I was completely taken aback by his friendly manner. Like Scrooge, I wondered if this was a setup.

"I'd like to give you this." The stranger held out a coffee mug with his company's name on the side. He didn't wait for my reply, but shouted "Merry Christmas" and sprinted away as fast as he dared on the slick pavement.

I stared after him, the coffee mug still in my hand. As the snow continued to fall steadily around me, a warm feeling spread throughout my body, and I smiled for the first time all day.

At home, that coffee mug serves as a constant reminder to me of the way that driver showed unexpected kindness and forgiveness to me that day. As I drink from it each day, it also reminds me of the way God forgives each of us when we least deserve it.

Using the coffee mug each morning as I begin my day inspires me to work on showing that same kindness and forgiveness to everyone I will meet—clerks, cashiers, complete strangers—not just at Christmas, but every day of the year.

Kayleen J. Reusser

A Gift Between Sisters

Over second and third cups flow matters of
high finance, high state, common gossip,
and low comedy.

New York Times, November 1949

I detected trepidation in my sister's voice over the
phone when she said, "Do you have a chair and a
cup of coffee handy? I need to ask you something."

A thousand possible scenarios crossed my mind as I
wrapped my Lake Michigan-icy hands around my favorite
stained coffee cup that boasts, "A good friend is like a good
bra. Hard to find, comfortable, supportive, and close to
your heart."

"Sure, go ahead," I said, not sure at all if I really wanted
to hear what she was about to say.

"I don't know how to say this except bluntly. Do you
have a kidney I could borrow?" Tammy said.

"Kidney, borrow? What are you talking about?"

Unbelievably, my sister, only two years older than me,
was dying at the age of forty-three. Tammy was in renal
kidney failure, and in order to survive she desperately
needed a kidney transplant. Her name was already on the
transplant waiting list, but her healthiest option would be

to receive a kidney from a live donor, and her best chance at survival would be a kidney from a sibling.

Without hesitation, I agreed to be her donor. If I could help her, I was willing, as I knew she would be for me.

Unlike most other sisters, Tammy and I did not have the opportunity to grow up together. We never had the chance to tell secrets in the dark after Mom and Dad said, "Lights out." Due to circumstances beyond our control, my sister and I were raised in separate foster homes. Except on rare occasions, we didn't have the opportunity to play in the park together, pushing each other on the swings or riding bicycles down the sidewalk. It had only been within the last few years, as adults, that we began sharing significant time together and growing, not only as sisters, but also as friends.

The day of the kidney transplant, we gave grief to the staff at Milwaukee's Froedtert Hospital as they prepared us for the surgery. Long-time coffee lovers, already without our favorite drink for twenty-four hours, we unsuccessfully pleaded for coffee through the IV. Eventually, a few days after the transplant, we were treated to a watered-down version of coffee. As my sister, alive and healthy, sat across from me with her steaming cup, we knew that the mocha water masquerading as coffee was the best cup of java we had ever had or will ever taste. During our hospital recovery, we shuffled to one another's rooms and shared our cravings for that elusive cup of really good coffee that we knew was in our future.

My sister is healthy today, and in the midst of busy lives taking care of family and careers, one thing we are certain to make time for are almost-daily phone calls over our cups of coffee. The aroma, the warmth, and the comfort of the coffee and the conversation are precious gifts of life and time spent together. Sometimes, you get a second chance.

Victoria Roder

Extra-HEARTy Blend

I don't have a problem with caffeine.
I have a problem without caffeine!

Author Unknown

aul had left for work without kissing me good-bye. Not a really big deal in the overall scheme of things, but I'd thought about it all the way to work. Of course, I could have initiated the smooch, but since he usually leaves before me, that is the last thing he does before he goes out the door.

When you've been married as long as we have, you learn to take things less seriously, but this had caused my antennae to go up. I knew he'd been traveling a lot lately, and I had been busy with my job, so I'd pushed any doubts about our relationship aside.

Now I wondered if we were growing apart. Was he taking me for granted? Was this just a bump in the road or a huge pothole?

With his long hours, Paul usually gets home long after I am asleep, so we don't usually get to talk at night. But we do take extra time each morning to linger over our coffee. That's when we catch up on details in each other's lives and take a moment to get in sync with each other. It's a special couple of minutes to say, "You matter to me."

The next morning over coffee, I tackled the problem head-on.

"Hey, babe, you know you forgot to kiss me good-bye yesterday. Anything in particular bothering you, or is there anything you want to talk about?"

"Nope, must have been in hurry." And with that he got up and went in the bathroom to shave.

I was really hurt. I expected a big hug, and I wanted to hear that we were "okay with each other" . . . that everything was fine between us. I wanted to know I still mattered in his life. I wanted reassurance that he still loved me. But I knew if I pushed, he would just resist.

I went to work with a heavy heart. He was my high-school sweetheart, my first love. I didn't want to lose our intimate moments, not even a simple kiss good-bye.

The weekend rolled around, and I knew Paul would want to stay home and relax. He'd been traveling twelve hundred miles a week as a West Coast salesman. I, on the other hand, being the one who worked in town all week, usually liked to go out on Saturday nights.

I would have to do some major cajoling to get Paul out of the house, but we needed to talk. And then I remembered his weakness and our strength—relaxing over a cup of joe.

"Hey, babe, would you like to join me for a cup of coffee, my treat?" I asked, holding my breath.

"I'm really tired, but . . . okay. If you drive, I guess I'm up for that."

That night as we sipped our coffee on the patio of

Starbucks, I found out that Paul's absentmindedness had nothing to do with me. He simply had a lot on his plate concerning his job. He explained he wanted to sort it out before talking to me about it. We cuddled, and he reassured me I was still his best girl. We giggled like teenagers who had found each other again. Paul was relieved to get his worries off his chest. I reassured him I was there for him and would be as supportive as I knew how. We hurried home to catch up on some long overdue smooching.

You can blame the entire evening on love, but I think it might have been the extra-HEARTY Moroccan blend we ordered. Whatever the reason, sometimes, it all comes down to the simple things in life, whether it's a kiss or a great cup of coffee.

Sallie A. Rodman

Ways to Brew the Bean:
Espresso

To make espresso, you'll need extremely fine, almost powdered, ground coffee through which nearly boiling water is forced under high pressure.

Espresso has a thicker consistency than drip coffee. A serving is measured in shots of about one ounce in size. It's designed to drink quickly because, once made, it degrades quickly from oxidation and loss of temperature.

The presence of crema, a reddish-brown foam that floats on the surface of the espresso, is its most unique feature. The crema is a combination of vegetable oils, proteins, and sugars.

The high-pressure brewing process concentrates all the flavors and chemicals so espresso lends itself to mixing with other coffee-based drinks such as cappuccino, latte, macchiato, and mocha without a loss of flavor.

Espresso contains twice the caffeine as regular brewed coffee.

The skeleton in My closet

Man does not live by coffee alone.
Have a danish.

Author Unknown

hen I was growing up, my family harbored a deep, dark secret. It haunted my elementary-school days, and just the thought of my teacher and my classmates learning this shameful secret sent icy shivers up and down my spine. What would they say if they ever learned that each morning for breakfast my family ate coffee soup?

True, we didn't all eat the same thing. Some of us put crackers in our coffee like my Uncle Bill, my father's bachelor uncle who lived with us, and some put bread in their coffee like my dad. And my sister Claire wouldn't touch coffee in any shape or form. But still . . .

I first learned that coffee soup wasn't the approved "breakfast of champions" when I was four years old and my sister Dot was born. At that time, babies were delivered at home, with the new mother remaining in bed for twelve days following the birth. This meant having a mother's helper come in to oversee the household, and so Flossie came to stay with us.

Taking our breakfast orders the first morning, Flossie

was appalled when we told her what we wanted.

"Coffee soup!" she exclaimed. "That's not a good break-fast for two little girls. Wouldn't you rather have milk soup instead?"

My older sister Ginny stuck to her guns. "Coffee soup," she said. But wanting to curry favor with Flossie, I capitulated.

"I'll try the milk soup," I told Flossie.

Even its appearance was yucky, with white, pallid chunks of bread floating in even whiter milk.

"Please," I begged Ginny after the first putrid mouthful, "trade with me. I'll let you have anything of mine you want if you'll just trade with me."

But Ginny was both adamant and smug. "You shouldn't have told her you wanted milk soup," she asserted. "You just did it to make Flossie like you. It serves you right."

When I was five years old, I had my tonsils removed. My parents, as did parents everywhere, emphasized the fact that I would be on a special diet following the surgery.

"Ice cream, anytime you want it, pudding, gelatin," my dad joked. "You're going to be just like a fairy princess, lying in bed with everyone hurrying to do your com-mands." The first day went fine.

The next morning I didn't want any gelatin, I didn't want any pudding, and I certainly didn't want any more ice cream. I wanted coffee soup. I threw a tantrum.

Finally, when all efforts to calm me had failed, my mother called our family doctor.

"If she's really that upset, give her the coffee soup," he advised. "All that screaming is probably doing her throat more harm than the crackers will."

The next year I began school, and I quickly realized that coffee soup was not part of the recommended breakfast diet.

For some reason I still cannot fathom, every year the teacher asked each student to name what they ate for breakfast. In a roomful of corn flakes and puffed-wheat eaters, I was not about to reveal my secret.

Instead, squirming in my seat and crossing my fingers, I mumbled "shredded wheat" when my turn came. But I knew I was living on borrowed time. My best friend Ilene, who lived two doors down from my house, was also in my class and knew the dreadful truth.

I had no illusions about Ilene's priorities. There was nothing she loved more than waving her hand and volunteering extraneous information to the class. Thanks to Ilene, we already knew her older sister Shirley not only chewed gum with her mouth open, but ate with her elbows on the table as well. And she wore boys' pajamas to bed!

If her own sister didn't inspire loyalty, what chance did I, a mere best friend, have? In this, I misjudged Ilene. In our six years of elementary school, she never outed me.

The Three Commandments of Coffee-Making

Thou shalt not over extract the oils from thy bean.
Thou shalt not boil thy coffee.
Thou shalt not reheat thy coffee.

Eventually, I did move on to other breakfast choices. But shredded wheat never became part of my breakfast fare.

In retrospect, I've concluded coffee soup was a carry-over from the Depression era, when the older generation made do with what little they had. And I've learned that coffee soup was neither as uncommon nor scandalous as I believed.

In fact, it was one of the memories my husband and I had in common.

Mary K. Young

Mister Coffee Blues

In Seattle, you haven't had enough coffee
until you can thread a sewing machine
while it's running.

Jeff Bezos

 few weeks ago, I said good-bye to old Mister Coffee, my morning companion of nearly sixteen years. I had been in denial for quite some time, wiping away embarrassing puddles on the counter, continually tightening his loose handle, and blaming his dark-stained filter basket on my aging dishwasher. I knew a geriatric coffeepot could have issues, but he continued to make the best coffee around, short of a Starbucks double latte.

When the glass carafe shattered and the only replacement I could find was a poorly fitting generic model, I knew Mister Coffee's days were numbered. It was time to face the truth—it was time to go shopping. I confess to a brief flirtation with other brands. I looked into a coffee machine that would grind my beans, but that was too messy. I checked out another that morphed into an espresso maker, but that was too expensive. I even had a one-morning fling with a bargain machine that brewed coffee so hot it seared my lips. It was back in the box and returned the next day. At that point, I thought about giving up coffee altogether. But in my heart, I knew Earl Grey and his herbal associates could never replace the fresh roasted flavor or the nose-tingling aroma that filled my kitchen every morning. So I went for broke. I pulled out my credit card and purchased a brand-new, state-of-the-art Mister Coffee.

The latest in small-appliance technology cost six times as much as his predecessor, but this new dude flaunted some impressive features. I was dazzled by his handsome tuxedo-style black-and-stainless shell and the tiny white numbers running up his twelve-cup indicator. I didn't even mind that he no longer fit in my appliance garage, or that he gurgled at the same decibel level as an idling bus. His luminescent green countdown timer merely enhanced my anticipation of that first morning cup.

There's just one problem—my spiffy new Mister Coffee is needy. Every two hours throughout the morning, he beeps several times and shuts down. To keep a steady stream of hot coffee flowing till noon, I must push "Select" and listen to another resounding chorus of beeps. On a busy day, when I'm facing a desk piled high with work and a dozen phone calls to return, I don't want to answer to a coffeepot. One more beep, and I'm ready to throw my new technologically advanced Mister Coffee across the room.

To be fair, the coffee is still dark brown and rich, and just as full-flavored as ever. But I find myself yearning for those silent coffee days when all I had to do was push the "On" button, when there was no risk of a cold cup. A time when one more demanding electronic device didn't rule my day. I've been rethinking my priorities lately. What's a few leaks and bad joints compared to the lack of peace and quiet? Any day now, I may be digging "dear old Dad" out of the small-appliance graveyard in my basement storage. So beep that, Mr. Fancy-Pants Coffee! Maybe there's something to be said for old age and experience after all.

Maureen Rogers

Approach with caution

I began wearing hats as a young lawyer
because it helped me to establish
my professional identity. Before that,
whenever I was at a meeting, someone
would ask me to get coffee.

Bella Abzug

am not a morning person. My husband and children wisely avoid me like the plague until they see
me in a state of caffeine-induced bliss. A few
months ago, the phone rang at 8:00 AM on a Saturday. No
one I know calls me that early on a weekend; they're smart.
I'm not a very pleasant person when awakened, especially
when I haven't had my java. Thinking it was a family emergency, I jumped out of bed and tripped over my shoes.

"This better be important," I grumbled as I limped down
the hallway to the phone. I reached the phone on the last
ring. "Hello," I panted.

"Yes. Is this Ms. Roppolo?" a nasal-sounding male voice
asked.

Who is this? I wondered. "This is Ms. Roppolo."

"Good morning. I'm calling to see if you would be interested in switching your long-distance service. You . . ."

"I'm not interested."

"If you would just stop being rude and interrupting, I'm sure we can find a package that suits your needs."

This solicitor calls me at eight in the morning, and I'm rude? I thought. I can't remember what I said, but I know it wasn't pleasant. By the time I got through telling the solicitor how I felt, he was tripping over his tongue in his haste to get off the phone with me.

A few days later, before my coffee was ready, I called the vet to get my dog spayed. A vet tech answered. I asked about the cost of spaying and was appalled at the price.

"Seventy-six dollars?" I yelped into the phone.

"No, thirty-six dollars." I was relieved. "Now, is your animal a dog or a cat?" she asked in a monotone voice.

Maybe it was the lack of caffeine, but I had no idea what she meant. "I-I'm sorry," I stammered. She sighed and repeated the question. The light bulb finally clicked on in my head. "Oh, a dog," I said proudly. A few minutes later, the tech hung up without saying good-bye. "Hmm. She must not have had any coffee either," I mused aloud.

That night, the family and I were talking about my mother staying at our house after her surgery. A few minutes later, we started talking about the dog's surgery. "The night before the surgery, we need to put her collar on and tie her up," I told John.

"She's just going to start hollering and wake the neighbors up," John pointed out. "I say we just put her in the garage."

"What if she makes a mess? You know how she loves magazines, and you have a stack of them in the garage."

"Easy, we just whack her with a newspaper. Speaking of messes . . . if she has an accident in the garage, I'll have to rub her nose in it," John said matter-of-factly. "That's how people used to do it."

I shook my head. "I can't do that; it's too cruel."

"Have it your way. She's your responsibility."

Evidently, our son Seth was unaware that the subject had changed from his grandmother to the dog. He stared at us in disbelief. "You are the cruelest people I've ever known. How could you put my granny in the garage?" I stared at Seth a few seconds before it dawned on me what he meant. I got a case of the giggles and collapsed on the floor laughing.

"Seth, baby," I gasped, "we're not talking about Granny. We're talking about the dog."

"Oh, leave me alone," he grumbled as he stalked out of the room. "I didn't have any caffeine today. I think I need a cup of coffee."

The old saying, "The apple doesn't fall far from the tree" or, in my case, "The cup doesn't stray far from the coffeepot," is true.

Debbie Roppolo

Java Jolt

Caffeine is a product of the type of bean, the ratio of water to coffee, and the brewing method used. It contributes nothing to the flavor of coffee, but the process of decaffeination changes the flavor and aroma. Ultimately, some caffeine still remains.

Per fluid ounce, regularly brewed coffee contains about 20 milligrams of caffeine compared to espresso's 40 milligrams. But because the average serving size for espresso is only one ounce, the amount of caffeine you consume is only about one-third the amount of a serving of regular brew.

USDA regulations require that in order to wear the label "decaffeinated," coffee must have had its caffeine level reduced by no less than 97.5 percent. Sounds impressive, doesn't it? Well, Arabica coffees are actually about 98 percent caffeine-free before any processing is done to lower the caffeine content. Consequently, most decafs are made with Robusta beans, which have a naturally higher caffeine level.

The most common method used to decaffeinate coffee requires beans to be soaked in water to dissolve the caffeine. Unfortunately, most of the compounds that are responsible for the flavor also fall victim to this soaking process. The caffeine is then extracted from the water by either solvents, such as methylene chloride and ethyl acetate, or through activated carbon. The beans are then re-soaked in the decaffeinated water to reabsorb some of the flavor compounds that were lost in the initial extraction.

An Expensive Pound of Coffee

Coffee makes us severe and grave
and philosophical.

Jonathan Swift

I was relatively new to the city, new to the snarling traffic, the parking challenges, and new to very fine coffee. My friend Rod, who is a connoisseur of coffee, had told me about Intelligentsia, located on the north side of Chicago. When I decided to check it out for myself, Rod gave me very specific directions, including advice to park across the street at the video store. As Rod directed, I pulled into the video parking lot, where I couldn't find metered parking. I paused briefly to look up at the faded parking guidelines painted on the brick wall, which warned that cars not belonging to video-store customers would be towed. But really, how could this possibly happen in five minutes, ten minutes tops?

Oh, my coffee-loving friends, by the time you order, wait for beans to be weighed, and leave the store with your steamy cup of complimentary brew, it can easily be the most expensive coffee you've ever tasted. I returned to my Toyota Corolla with a spring in my step, my pound of coffee in the shop's trendy bag in one hand, my cup of coffee in the other. As I moved to the driver's side, it was as if I had hit the brick wall bearing the faded parking warning. On its left rear tire, my dear old Toyota wore a bright yellow boot, the kind reserved for "parking felons"—those people who I imagine just throw their parking tickets into the wind, or rip them into shreds with nary a lawful care.

But here was a boot, and a very nasty "booter" to whom I now tearfully pleaded my case. He sat in an old black sedan, night and day I imagine, doing this to nice people like me. He led me to the sign and told me in no uncertain terms that it would cost $75 to have the mechanical boot removed. Then he topped off my afternoon with some abusive attitude and words that can't be shared on these pages.

So I did the only thing I could do: I walked two blocks and crammed my cash card into the ATM to withdraw the money I only hoped was in my meager bank account. After I paid the booter, I drove away, still shaking and full of both anger and relief, feeling as though I'd just posted bail for a crime I didn't commit—or at least one for which the punishment didn't fit the crime. I spent the next day making phone calls and drafting a letter—mostly about the guy's behavior—to the video store, the coffee shop, the alderman, and the towing company. It took months, a year actually, for me to return to this particular coffee shop. Friends would offer to pick me up coffee when they went there, knowing it was a sore subject.

Then a story caught my attention a few months back about a new Intelligentsia coffee selling for $103.90 a pound. (It works out to four cents a bean in case you care about such details.) Outrageous! Unbelievably, they sold out of that particular blend. This was just the news to pique my curiosity and entice me to return. When I ventured back, I had to smile. The video-store parking lot had been turned into public parking with a minimum rate of one dollar for a half-hour. Sounds perfect for a quick run-in to get a $100-pound of coffee.

Julie B. Sevig

Gift of the Peppermint Mocha, Low-Fat Magi

We would take something old and tired and
we would rediscover the mystique and
charm that had swirled around coffee
throughout the centuries.

Howard Schutz

He greets me every morning from behind the coffee counter. Often, it feels like he and I are the only two human beings alive at the ungodly hour of 6:00 AM. At that time, in the dead of winter, it's still dark outside, sometimes rainy and almost always cold. Faced with an hour-long commute to my job, I schlep into the coffee shop in a semi-vegetative state. I need that jolt of caffeine to wake me up, especially when I've stayed up too late the night before, hooked on a Law & Order marathon or anxious to finish reading, for the third time, *A Tree Grows in Brooklyn*.

My coffee guy is always smiling, always cheerful, even though the counter he works behind is just yards away from the front door and subjects him to cold winter winds each time a customer enters the shop. This store is a franchise, and he's not the owner. He's just a college student and probably earns minimum wage at best. Still, he greets each customer like a long-lost family member. I never need to remind him what my favorite drink is or how I like it prepared. The minute I enter the shop, he smiles and calls out, "The same?" When I nod, he immediately begins preparing my peppermint mocha, extra hot (nuclear, he calls it), with low-fat milk and just a smidge of whipped crème.

Sometimes, I'll also buy a chai tea latte for my mom and swing by her house since I pass it on my way to work. When I do this, my coffee guy gives me the 50 percent senior's discount on her drink, even though he has no way of knowing if I'm really buying it for a senior or I'm just a double-fisted drinker. Once he chased after me in the store parking lot to let me know I had earned a free coffee with the store's frequent-buyer card. He apologized because he had forgotten to honor it and wanted to let me know my next coffee was free.

These are all minor gestures, but collectively they add up to great customer service. And that's why I wanted to thank my coffee guy at Christmas time. "What can I buy somebody whom I know nothing about?" I asked my manager. She shrugged. "He may not even celebrate Christmas," she reminded me. "A Christmas gift may not be appropriate."

True. Still, I had to let him know that his kindness frequently sets the tone for my day. Every morning, I return to my car with my extra-hot, low-fat peppermint mocha in hand, warmed by his attentiveness and touched by his kindness.

"Maybe he has a thing for you," my manager teased. But I quickly dismissed the notion. My coffee guy can't be a day over twenty-one. I could easily be his much, much older sister. No, this wasn't about attraction, trying to score points, schmoozing or anything else. He was just a kind person. And I wanted to say thank-you.

I finally decided on a gift card to a local book and record store. Surely, he could find something there to enjoy. I tucked the gift in a safely generic "Happy Holidays" card and wrote inside, "Thank you for the cheerful attitude and great customer service you provide year-round." I signed it, The Peppermint Mocha Latte Lady.

Christmas Eve morning, I arrived at the shop at my usual ungodly hour, but not in my typical bleary-eyed state. I was a tad giddy with anticipation, excited to brighten my coffee guy's day just as he had so often brightened mine. While he was making my peppermint mocha, I snuck the card alongside the register where he'd be sure to find it after I left.

As he handed me my drink, he told me to wait a second. Then he reached underneath the counter and handed me a gift-wrapped box of chocolates with a card. "I just want to say thanks," he stammered with an awkward smile. What? He was thanking ME? Then, because he could see I was speechless, he wished me a happy holiday and returned to his growing line of customers.

In the pre-dawn dark of my car, I flicked on the light and opened the envelope. It was a Christmas card. Inside was printed, "A Christmas wish to show you just how nice it is to know you." He had added, "Thank you for always being so nice. It makes our job easy, especially when everyone else is so grumpy. Merry Christmas."

I thought of the card I'd left behind, tucked behind his register, and couldn't help but smile.

It was a very mocha Christmas indeed.

Eileen Mitchell

Watch Out for Tea Lovers!

Forever: the time it takes to brew
the first pot of coffee in the morning.

Author Unknown

 love coffee, any kind of coffee, as long as it's not too strong, too weak, too old, or espresso.

My husband, on the other hand, is an espresso maniac. Despite high blood pressure, a cranky disposition, and limited financial resources, he buys espresso coffee by the truckload. Our freezer contains Café Busto espresso, Kona Estates espresso, Colombian espresso, Nicaraguan espresso, Nigerian espresso, and North Dakota espresso. He could start a store. I tell him I have dibs on dying first because I do not want to have to drink all that he will leave behind.

On the other hand, my daughter is a tea freak. Her cupboards are as full of tea as our freezer is of espresso. She is a missionary for tea. "Mom, coffee is not good for you," she says.

"Tell your father," I say as she dumps a soggy tea bag into my coffee cup.

"He won't listen," she says.

"Really?" I say.

But maybe, I decide, she is right. The Red Cross nurse at the blood bank told me last Thursday that my blood pressure was marginal. "You'd better watch that," she said. "You're one of our regulars, but you won't be able to give anymore if your pressure goes any higher." Now, that would be a tragedy. I just love wearing that little sticker that says, "Be nice to me—I gave blood today." Nobody ever obeys it, but the message is comforting.

So, I decide, my daughter is right. Tea.

"Green tea," she decides. "You look old. Green has lots of antioxidants, you know."

I look old. Great. I love you, too.

"Green tea?" the clerk at Shop 'n Save asks. "What's that?" She looks old, too.

The next time Dear Daughter comes from New Jersey, she brings green tea, boxes of it. Her back seat is filled with it. She leaves her suitcases in the front hall. She does not even take off her coat. She boils the water—no microwaving of tea water for her! She puts a bag of Barry's Green Tea in my cup. ("The real thing," she says. I did not know that tea grows in Ireland.) She pours the water. I watch the water turn pale green. It smells pretty good. I wait for the boil bubbles to die down, and I take a sip. Not bad, I decide. I drink a whole cup of green tea.

I drink another. And another (new bag). And one more. I am looking younger every minute.

Three and a half minutes after my fourth cup of green tea, my left upper arm begins to itch. Strange.

Then my right arm. Worse than strange. Then my upper back and the inside of my right thigh. "Your face looks funny," my tea-drinking daughter observes.

I feel funny.

I go to the bathroom and look in the mirror. I have the measles. Chicken pox. Scarlet fever. I do look younger, though—like a child who has contracted six kinds of kid diseases.

Well, to summarize, my body is one large—old—bundle of rash. I have rash on the soles of my feet. I have rash in my hair. I have rash in places I didn't know could rash. And I itch.

The pharmacist smiles tightly, very tightly because he is having a difficult time not laughing. "Yup," he says, "must have been something you ate." He does laugh. "Either that," he says, "or you're allergic to air."

"Ha, ha, ha," I say. "Give me that cortisone spray. Give me six bottles of that cortisone spray. Charge it to my husband." He, too, after one look at me, has been laughing.

I open the first bottle of spray before I am even in sight of my car. I think of drinking it, but I control myself, close my eyes, and spray my face. Ahh! Right there on the sidewalk, I spray my hands. I start spraying my legs before I get the car door closed.

I don't care anymore. Coffee. Latte, cappuccino, betel nut, ginger peachy, even espresso if I'm really desperate and can hold my nose. High blood pressure or no high blood pressure, Red Cross or no Red Cross, daughter or no daughter—I'm back to coffee.

Barbara Smith

Coffee Cups

The morning cup of coffee has an
exhilaration about it which the
cheering influence of the afternoon
or evening cup of tea cannot be
expected to reproduce.

Oliver Wendell Holmes, Sr.

T raditionally in my northern Italian family, after the
women reached "dignita," or possessed of dignity,
which meant some age after fifty-five, they'd
acquire a china cup, quite unceremoniously and unan-
nounced. While I never considered them old, this cup business seemed to be akin to an unspoken rite of passage to
some state of mind, some point in life, some level. Special.

As a child, I was completely annoyed and puzzled by
my Nonna's attachment to her cup and coffee rituals.
When the instant kind came out, the women would refuse
it, even if it was the only offering. It had to be brewed,
boiled, or pressed, strong and robust, laced with two teaspoons of sugar. They were suspicious of people who
made "weak" coffee.

Nonna took her "later in the day" cuppa in "the cup,"
not the thick white, chipped mug she used for her sunrise

cuppa. The cup was covered with delicate violets, her life-long hallmark. Even more puzzling was the deep, mysterious attitude she'd adopt when using it. She'd sit quietly and motionless, deep in thought, holding it under her nose, while staring out the window. When drinking, she'd inhale the aroma, eyes half-closed, humming, "Da caffè's good today." Her little finger, slightly crooked, was poised like a half butterfly, pointing upward. Any efforts on my part for her attention during this mind-and-cup meld were met with the slight and slow turn of the head, and the black stare of a killer shark.

At some point, a china cup showed up in my aunt's kitchen. Her cup had pink apple blossoms. She was a tiny, delicate, and feminine woman. Then came my mother's lily-of-the-valley. She loved the grace of the flower, and that female saints were often depicted holding a bunch, traits she'd always wanted and had never attained. She was much too lively. All the women held the china cups the same way, dainty butterfly finger accompanied by that faraway look. They took special pains to wash, dry, and carefully put them out of harm's way. On occasion, I was required as the coffee slave to find, fetch, and fill them for my mother. The whole ritual was an aromatic bore, but, while delivering the product, I'd make the repeated pitch.

"So—what's so special?" I'd ask her. Sometimes I'd get an answer instead of a sharp look, but it was always the same.

"You're too young to understand," she'd say wistfully. "Someday, you will."

Through the years, relatives, friends, and spouses

bought each woman cups, even started collections for them. But they were placed on what-not shelves unused. There was just that one favorite. As each woman passed away, the cups disappeared.

Several summers ago, while on a trip through the South, I found myself looking for a cup in all those wonderful out-of-the-way places tucked in small towns. I found one in Arkansas. It was paper-thin and painted with English wildflowers—bluebells, delphiniums, roses, forget-me-nots, and bright yellow daisies. I cherish the wild, high alpine meadows struck with those gifts when I'm hiking in my New Mexico home state.

In the way of the women in my family, I drink from no other—finger crooked and poised like a butterfly, inhaling the aroma. I stare off into the distance with that faraway look I remember so well. I know the secret of their thoughts now.

I think of the time past, because I have enough past to think of. I can forgive myself my many mistakes raising my daughters, take joy in my life, miss Nonna, my mother, my aunt, and see now the enormous gifts they gave me. I embrace the road backward, comforted by my choices, and look forward to the future, strengthened by those enduring women who have gone before me. I count my blessings, know I am loved, and love in return. In those deeply personal and cherished solitary moments, I think of my husband, children, friends, life, and feel rich beyond measure, drinking that richness from my own special cup. I know it represents one beautiful, irreplaceable, and fragile thing—my own life. I have lived it well, given of myself, tried hard, fallen down, risen, and rebuilt so many times. It's those very difficult places that have given me my dignity, but the beloved women in my life showed me the way to bear them.

I found and bought my cup for myself, no other. I do not share it with anyone. It was not a necessary expense, but I have spent years buying the necessary and the exquisite for everyone else in my life. This cup represents a "me first" declaration every day. I chose it completely on my own. I did not ask anyone's opinion or permission. I care for it myself. Different from my mother, I do not require that my daughters become coffee slaves, but, on occasion, they bring me a cuppa. And so does my husband—on the weekends, in bed, along with the paper.

One day, the cup will go back out into the world and will not belong to my daughters or granddaughters. They will find one on their own.

Isabel Bearman Bucher

Caffeine Fiend: A Dark Roast

Almost all my middle-aged and elderly
acquaintances, including me, feel about
twenty-five, unless we haven't had our coffee, in which case we feel 107.

Martha Beck

W ednesday morning, 6:00 am. My mindless morning routine followed its familiar course as I
plowed a furrow into my chilly kitchen: first
dump soggy, swollen grounds in trash, replace filter,
measure just enough (plus an extra shot) of Colombian
extra dark, spoon grounds in the brew basket, fill reservoir
with filtered water, press the "On" button . . . press the . . .
press . . .

"Noooooo!" I heard my own pathetic voice echo in the
early-morning darkness. "Not this morning! Don't die
now! Please. I need you!"

Over and over, I depressed the coffee maker's "On" button like a shoddy actress desperately urging a dying lover.
"No! It can't be! You were fine only yesterday! You're too
new to die. You're only what . . . five, maybe six years old?
That's mid-life in coffee-maker years!"

Pulse. Pulse. Pulse. I attempted to revive the small

appliance using a demented version of CPR (Coffee Percolator Resuscitation). Frantically, my glazed-over eyes searched the kitchen for a cause of appliance failure. Could my Mister Coffee (affectionately named Joe) simply be unplugged? Clogged? Pressing my ear against Joe's heart, I strained to hear just one gurgle. One familiar hiss. "There! Could it be? No . . ." It was only the nearby refrigerator, alive and breathing, its hum low and steady.

I had to face reality. Joe had flat-lined. Clamoring down the hall to our bedroom, I shook my sleeping husband like a limp dishrag. "Honey! Wake up! It's an emergency! Joe died! Only you can help!" My husband yawned, rolled up in our bed sheets, and snored. Through my groggy fog, I suddenly had a revelation. It occurred to me that my husband had never really liked Joe. Said he was too slow to brew. Dripped too much. Made that really loud sucky noise.

Hmmmmmm. "You killed Joe!" I ranted, stripping the sheets off my husband like an old Band-Aid. Ouch. "You always hated that coffee maker! You wanted some newfangled espresso machine!" I accused my half-asleep husband. I then transformed into a creature straight out of War of the Worlds. Fire spat out of my greedy eyes. Venom dripped from my addict-twitching lips. Inches from my husband's sluggish face, I seethed, "I . . . can't . . . have . . . coffee!" The drowsy, half-naked man in the bed lifted his tired lids just enough to respond, "Maybe we [yawn] blew a fuse."

Relieved, I stood up and took a single cleansing breath. Then I purred, "Fuse? A fuse! That's logical. So it can be fixed? Preferably just in time for my whole–wheat, cinnamon-raisin toast to pop up?"

Rolling out of bed, my sweet husband trudged down the basement stairs. Ten minutes later, he found me lounging on the deck in my Adirondack chair enjoying a brilliant magenta sunrise. Sipping a strong, dark brew out of my favorite mug (which incidentally reads, "Behind every successful woman is a substantial cup of coffee"), I gazed lovingly at my husband. Sauntering up to me like a hero from an old Western, he planted a gentle kiss on my rosy cheek. As I batted my eyelashes at him, I asked, "Honey, did you recognize that pathetic woman who clamored through the house this morning babbling nonsense about killing her coffee maker?"

"What woman?" my husband responded, planting on me another of his clean-shaven kisses. "I have no idea who that woman was. I only hope, though, that a certain pathetic, caffeine-crazed woman never comes face-to-face with a certain pathetic football-fan guy who loses his remote control during the big game. Now that . . . would be dark."

Cristy L. Trandahl

Who Wants to Go First?

Kopi Luwak is a highly prized, top-grade coffee and one of the most expensive in the world. It is a rich, smooth coffee with an earthy, syrupy texture and a hint of chocolate undertones. In the Philippines, only 1,100 pounds of Luwak coffee are produced each year. Supply and demand drive the prices well into the hundreds of dollars per pound.

What makes Kopi Luwak so special? You'll never guess! The Indonesian islands are home to a nocturnal, tree-climbing catlike animal known as a civet (Luwak). They prowl coffee plantations at night, picking and consuming the finest ripened coffee cherries. Each morning, after the cherries have passed through the civet, they are collected from the animal's droppings.

The beans emerge without their fleshy coating, but whole. They are washed and carefully cleansed before being processed. Research suggests that the beans are slightly digested during their passage. Speculation is that an enzyme process breaks down some of the proteins, resulting in a less bitter coffee, or that a lactic-acid fermentation may be a factor. Laboratory attempts at mimicking nature have so far failed.

Kopi Luwak is available from specialty importers in the United States or can be purchased online directly from the growers and processors in Indonesia.

To make a perfect cup of coffee from your beans—Indonesian style—place one-half teaspoon of finely ground beans in a cup, pour boiling water over the coffee, stir and allow it to settle before drinking. Bon appétit!

Mocha Madness

In my next life, I want to be tall and thin,
be able to parallel park, and
make good coffee.

Paula Danziger

"Want a mocha?" my husband asks, turning left into the parking lot of a Starbucks.

Do I want an exquisite mix of espresso, steamed milk, and chocolate sliding down my throat? "No," I say, my voice as firm as I can manage.

"You're going to pass up a mocha? I'll even buy," Ray says, inching our Prius between an Explorer and a Honda SUV.

He's in a generous mood, and ordinarily I'd take advantage of it. But even if I order a nonfat, no-whip, I'm still in for a lot of calories. It won't take too many more mochas to move me into a larger dress size.

"One can't hurt," he says. His unspoken message is that if I cave in along with him—he's theoretically on a diet, too—we'll not only get drinks, but we'll split a pastry as well. He adores nearly any pastry.

He's cruel to push me. I can't be strong very long. For years, I didn't drink any kind of coffee. Didn't care for the taste, believe it or not. I didn't like coffee anything, from mud pie to tiramisu. Then I discovered mochas. The last ten pounds is history.

"Chocolate's good for you, you know." Ray is pulling out his big guns. Sinners like company. Yes, I've heard the argument that a small amount of dark chocolate every day is good for us. I think it's two tablespoons. What is the equivalent in Italian chocolate syrup?

And much as I love mochas, I can't really defend their value to my health. My physical health anyway. I can't put a mocha on one side of a balance scale, a plate of fresh veggies on the other, and expect equilibrium. Although, come to think of it, I do consider them excellent for my mental health.

Theoretically, since I like mochas so much, I could have a short mocha now and then and cut back on other carbs, saturated fats, and sugar. Since it's a simple matter of calories, I could sit down and figure it all out. But I haven't yet, so today I'd better go without. Come on, girl, I think to myself. Show a little will power. Surely, I can be stronger than a hot—or sometimes cold—coffee drink.

I fortify myself with the thought that if I don't buy mochas, I'll save money. Ray is paying today, but usually it's my debit card that I pass across the counter. If I go entirely without mochas for a month, I'll save enough to buy a new shirt or get a pedicure. Six months and I can treat us to a weekend at the coast. I picture a quiet beach, water lapping at my bare ankles, red sun setting on a tranquil ocean. In my imagination, I take Ray's hand and lift my face to kiss his cheek. What could be better than a moment of pure romance?

Ray grips the door handle. Clicks it open. The sound shatters my reverie. Will it be a beach romance, or a drink seductive as a warm summer night, smooth as suede, satisfying as a delicious book? "I do want a mocha," I cry, clutching his arm. "Grande. Brève. No whip."

Samantha Ducloux Waltz

"We're coffee aficionados. This is our son—Juan Valdez."

Reprinted by permission of Jonny Hawkins. ©2007 Jonny Hawkins.

They're Not Here for the Coffee

Coffee: we can get it anywhere, and get
as loaded as we like on it, until such teeth-
chattering, eye-bulging, nonsense-gibbering
time as we may be classified unable
to operate heavy machinery.

Joan Frank

I t's a rare morning off for me, and I take advantage of the opportunity to go for a brisk walk at the mall. On the way home, I stop at McDonald's for breakfast. As I enter the dining room, I blink in surprise. The restaurant is nearly filled with members of the senior set. Silver-haired couples are sitting across from each other, some with the smiles of newlyweds. At other tables, clusters of men are teasing one another and swapping stories. They're the regulars here; I am the outsider. I've walked into a vibrant society rarely seen by us 9-to-5ers— the senior coffee-house community.

"Hey, Chuck, what do you know?" one ruby-cheeked fellow says.

"Not much," Chuck says, peeling off his coat before sitting at the booth. He completes a foursome of men around the table. "How 'bout you?"

"Can't complain. Wouldn't do any good if I did." They drink coffee and dig into their breakfast sandwiches.

"Did you lose your electric after that storm last night?"

"For a couple of hours. And you?"

Up at the counter, I'm waiting for my order, and another gentleman comes up with his coffee cup in hand. "Hey there, Mary. You keeping out of mischief?"

The young server smiles. "Yep. Haven't got time for mischief."

He shakes his head as he pours himself a cup. "Too bad." He chuckles at his own joke. On the way back to his table, he waves at a couple. The man and woman both grin at him and wave back.

Fifty years ago, these folks would have been hailing each other at the local bar or at a civic meeting. They might have chatted at the park while their children played or bowled together on a league. Today, they're sharing their time in a fast-food restaurant. But they're not here for the senior discount. And the coffee refills are nice, but that's not what brought them here. They're here for the community they have formed by choosing to be regulars.

If Chuck didn't come in for his cup of coffee that morning, one of his buddies would be sure to give him a call. His children may have moved away, but his friends are there at the new watering hole to ask about his day and to know how he's doing. They listen to his stories and laugh at his jokes, the way friends do. They can be counted on to sympathize with his griefs and to rejoice with his joys. And he does the same for them.

On those mornings, that place ceases to be just another

fast-food restaurant on the strip. It becomes a sanctuary. With the world outside and good companions inside, the regulars here can be themselves and enjoy each other's company. I was the only person alone at a table that day, but that was okay. I was glad for them that they were not alone. They may have first come to McDonald's seeking breakfast and a cup of coffee, but they found much more. They joined a community of friends.

Debra Weaver

In Good Company

A 2006 poll conducted by the Specialty Coffee Association of America revealed some interesting demographics about coffee and our culture.

Sixteen percent of adults in the United States drink coffee every day. That's more than 300 million cups of coffee, and 75 percent of those cups are home-brewed.

By the end of 2006, there were over 19,000 cafes or kiosks in the United States specializing in coffee, and they represented nearly $10 billion in annual sales. Over 2,000 retailers actually roast the beans on the premises.

Seventy percent of coffee drinkers ranked coffee quality and a convenient location as the most important factor in deciding on which coffee house to patronize. A friendly, knowledgeable staff came in second on the list at 40 percent, followed by variety (35 percent) and price (26 percent).

Memories to Be Treasured

Black coffee must be strong and very hot;
if strong coffee does not agree with you,
do not drink black coffee. And if you
do not drink black coffee,
do not drink any coffee at all.

André Simon

My elderly Aunt Ann was a special lady to me. She paid for my college education at a time when my father was struggling with a job loss and Mom was our only wage earner. That meant that I graduated from college without the burden of student loans. When I asked Aunt Ann why she had been so generous, she simply shrugged and looked beyond me, like she was gazing at some old memories.

"I never had kids of my own," she finally said, flashing a gentle smile. Her hands picked up her needlework, and she began to stitch. "I guess I wanted to be a blessing to Peg's daughter." Peg was my mom, and Aunt Ann was actually my Mom's aunt and my great-aunt. She was long retired from her secretarial job with the power company, and she had saved her money all those years since. I was mighty impressed that she had chosen to share her bounty with me.

"I owe you a lot," I ventured to say, but she waved her wrinkled hand in the air to stop my expression of thanks.

"We should always try to be a blessing to others," she advised with conviction. "Especially the next generation." She sighed. "You young people can carry on doing what we can't do anymore."

That was so like Aunt Ann, to think of others before herself. Before arthritis had crippled her legs and forced her to stop her volunteer work, she'd maintained and lived in her own house. Due to mobility concerns, Mom and Dad insisted that she move in with us in our suburban residence. I'd just graduated from college and was living at home while searching for employment. Every morning, I'd watch as Aunt Ann would come out of her bedroom on the ground floor, using her walker to make the slow trek from her bedroom, through the living room to our kitchen. She and I would sit and have breakfast together after everyone else had already left for work.

Aunt Ann loved her morning coffee and breakfast rolls. That became my unofficial function in the household—to stop by the bakery twice a week and stock up on pastry. Her favorite was the German-style stollen with its butter-rich dough, cherries, pineapple, almonds, and raisins. I loved the swirl cinnamon coffee cake that could be broken off in chunks, which I plastered with fresh butter and wolfed down with gusto.

We always complemented these goodies with mugs of steaming dark coffee. As Aunt Ann relaxed and commented on stories in the morning paper, I'd get the coffeepot going. I'd measure out heaping spoonfuls of a mountain-grown specialty blend into the old-fashioned percolator-style pot. To this day, I can see the white porcelain container with a sprig of blue flowers imprinted on the side. Adding a dash of salt to the mixture for taste, I'd plunk the lid back on, then relax in a hard-backed chair and munch on breakfast rolls as we waited for that rich brew to finish percolating.

"Das schmeckt so gut," Aunt Ann would sigh after taking her first gulp of my coffee. I knew enough of her old-country lingo to know the phrase meant, "That tastes so good." I wanted to please her in this one small way, and her approval of my effort always made me feel worthwhile. I felt like I was being a blessing back to her, in return for all she had done for me. It was one singular but significant way I could show her I cared.

Truth to tell, our first cup of coffee together each morning invigorated us with more than its own distinctive taste. Along with the cornucopia of fine coffees we tried during those special breakfasts, I realized that the two of us were also sharing memories. And now, as I look back on those days decades later, I appreciate the time we had together, now that all I have of my dear relative and mentor Aunt Ann is a photo in a frame on my kitchen counter.

In my opinion, no breakfasts before or since ever tasted so good.

Cheryl Elaine Williams

Smells Like Love

A leaf fluttered in through the window
this morning, as if supported by the rays
of the sun, a bird settled on the fire
escape, joy in the task of coffee, joy
accompanied me as I walked.

Anaïs Nin

ertain smells and sounds have the power to take us back to a place and time where we felt safe and truly at home. Coffee does that for me. And what comes to mind is an old percolator. In our household, things did not always go perfectly. Some nights after I went to bed, there were arguments, and as a child these frightened me. But then morning would come.

My mother and father would get up very early. Dad worked in construction, and his days often started before the sun came up. Often I would wake up in the predawn dark and hear them getting ready. I would lie there, cuddled in my bed, lazy and warm. That early, the entire world seemed still, and I would listen to the gentle sounds of drawers being pulled out and then closed, of closet doors quietly being opened and shut, and to the sounds of my mother going to the kitchen to get breakfast ready for my dad.

But before all this, the first sound I heard was the coffee percolator that had been readied the night before. I awoke to the gurgling sound of the water rising in the pipe and bubbling in the glass lid. The coughing, wheezing sound of the water as it filtered down into the basket was music to my ears. I knew that as my mother entered the kitchen, the coffee would be ready, a strong brew that my father favored, and she would pour that first cup for my father so it would be just right when he came in for his breakfast. I would lie there as long as possible, soaking all of it up: the aroma, the warmth, the feeling of contentment. I would listen to the sound of safety and love talking quietly to each other just a few feet away.

Then I would hear the footsteps of my mother as she would come down the hall, gently open my door, and let me know it was time to get up and start the day. And I would know that we were all okay, and my world had come together again.

My modern-day kitchen boasts all the modern conveniences, including, of course, a coffee maker. But none of the gadgets makes me feel so safe, so secure, as that old percolator did so many years ago.

Theresa Theiler

Coffee at Pike Place

He was my cream, and I was his coffee—
and when you poured us together,
it was something.

Josephine Baker

 our potted raspberry vines stared accusingly at me, but I managed to ignore them as I made my way to the car. My friend's invitation was too tempting. "I'm heading north today. Want to meet for coffee?"

I needed a break. I needed to lay off the cooking, baking, cleaning, planting, and harvesting, and steal a few hours of walking, shopping, talking, and laughing. So no, I didn't feel the least bit guilty as I walked past those pots. The raspberries could wait. We'd settled on the Pike Place Market as a good halfway spot to meet for coffee.

Once there, it took some doing to actually connect. After no less than six cell-phone calls back and forth, we found each other, hugged hello, and ducked into the first pastry shop we spotted.

A room full of warm, just-from-the-oven bread . . . and rolls . . . and tarts . . . and quiche . . . and puff pastry enveloped us. Add to that the aroma of French Roast drip and espresso, the sounds of frothing milk and chatter, and chairs scooching toward tables, ahhh . . . pure bliss.

After perusing the pastry cases, Sandra ordered something twisted, glazed, and nut-studded. As I'm not a sweets-in-the-morning person, I ordered a Swiss-cheese-encrusted square of puff pastry—a concoction so light, so tender, it shattered into flaky particles with every bite. I could have eaten twelve.

We asked for our coffee in real cups, not paper. Sandra took hers black, but I ordered my signature latte. And oh, how superior that latte was to my usual franchise-on-every-corner cup! I feel deceitful even thinking such a thought, let alone writing it, but how can you not 'fess up to something so blatant? The froth was so thick it coated the sides of my cup.

Each tip to my lips, each movement of my wrist, created a new pattern of cream and brown swirls across the surface of that decadent brew. The tendrils of steam that rose from its midst were so potently rich, I couldn't stop sniffing.

Sandra and I are writer friends. I write for adults; she writes for children. On occasion, we've taught at writers' conferences together. Both our husbands are in the ministry. Because we live nearly two hours apart, we rarely see each other. So with several months of catching up to do, you can probably imagine the animated scene at our table.

We talked first about writing, and the projects we're each mulling over, and the difficulties of balancing family needs and contracted writing obligations. We shared the happenings at my church and at her husband's retirement center, and discussed the particular bittersweet nature of being pastors' wives, and about our strong desire to model grace to the women we minister to.

With little effort at all, we sipped and laughed and talked away an hour. Had we parted then, it would have been enough for me. I would have had the gulp of fresh, courage-endowing air I'd come looking for. But we didn't part.

We meandered through the market comparing the bouquets of statice and just-cut lovelies that adorned about every third booth, sampling glossy chocolates, listening to the street musicians, watching the fishmongers toss salmon back and forth, and enjoying their jovial bellows. We ogled at people and the jeweled mounds of fruits and vegetables displayed like artwork.

Sandra bought a jar of sour cherry jam, a half-pound of pickled red onions, and five Southern-fried chicken pieces that she vowed to save for dinner. I bought a pound of Brussels sprouts, three pounds of creamy Yukon potatoes, and an autumn bouquet of burgundy zinnias, butter-yellow lilies, orangey-red sunflowers, and golden black-eyed Susans.

Just before we said our good-byes, I picked up a warm sleeve of Epis (braided rolls), which balanced my arms nicely.

"Let's meet for coffee," my friend had suggested. And, as always, the promise implied by that invitation hadn't disappointed. Coffee has a power nothing else can quite match.

We don't meet for Brussels sprouts, flowers, or pickled red onions. We meet for coffee, and somewhere amidst all that sipping and sniffing, coffee works its magic. It relaxes shoulders, sends tension skedaddling, and coaxes smiles back in place. Over the course of one cup, hearts open. And sometimes, hearts are healed. That's one mighty powerful cup.

Shannon Woodward

Drying Out

Beans start out at about 60 percent moisture content. Before shipment, they must be dried to no more than 11 percent.

In Brazil, and to a lesser degree in Central America, coffee is typically dried on large asphalt or cement patios in long shallow rows. Patio drying helps accelerate the drying process, and prevents fermentation and moldy beans from developing. Next to each row is open ground, which has been warmed and dried by the sun. Every half-hour, the coffee is shifted into the dry rows. This shifting continues for 6-7 days for washed (wet-processed) coffees and 12-14 days for natural (dry-processed) coffees.

A moisture meter is used to measure the moisture content, and when it reaches about 15 percent, the coffee is moved to mechanical dryers to finish the process. This last few percent is the slowest part of the coffee-drying process, and in environments with high humidity, the entire drying process takes place in mechanical dryers.

In Africa, most coffee is dried by using drying tables. This is the best, but least utilized, method of drying coffee.

Here the pulped and fermented coffee is spread in thin sheets on raised beds, which allow air to pass on all sides of the coffee. The drying coffee is mixed by hand. This process results in a more uniform drying and less fermentation.

A relatively new method of drying is the use of solar coffee dryers. They are more economical than mechanical dryers that are powered by fuel or electricity, and they are more efficient than patio drying. Unfortunately, despite these advantages, they are not widely used.

Coffee Talk

Ah! How sweet coffee tastes!
Lovelier than a thousand kisses,
sweeter far than muscatel wine!

J. S. Bach

My passion for coffee first brewed at age five when Grandma Anna poured the warm golden-brown magic into my cup. It all began at our kitchen table, where Grandma's Swedish friends gathered for their kaffe kalas or coffee parties. Elsa, Mia, Ellen, and Linnea always brought baked goods to share, and Grandma often baked a batch of her famous Swedish cardamom rolls. I was the official greeter, and couldn't wait to find my place at the table to discover the delicacies that awaited me. The idea that coffee would stunt my growth was never heard in my home.

My cup contained Anna's special Swedish blend egg coffee. During those early years, my cup was filled with part cream, part coffee, and a sugar cube. Later, I discovered Grandma's recipe. It was a mixture of ground coffee, beaten egg, and cold water, stirred into a pot of boiling water. The heat was turned off, and more cold water was added. It stood about ten minutes until the grounds settled. Sometimes a crushed eggshell was added to the mixture. The result was a coffee pure, clear, golden-brown in color, and smooth to the taste. I can still smell the rich aroma of that golden-brown coffee, and I carry it with me in my memories.

I remember being puzzled the first time I saw Grandma add eggshell to the mixture. "Grandma, I don't think I'll like the coffee with eggshells," I told her one morning. "Will I be able to taste them? Will they hurt my tongue?"

"My little sweet grandchild," said Grandma Anna, "don't worry about the eggshells. They will blend with the coffee grounds and settle to the bottom of the pot. You'll never know they were there."

Grandma Anna always sucked on a sockerbit (sugar cube) as she daintily sipped her coffee. If my coffee was too hot, Anna allowed me to pour some carefully into the cup's saucer and sip the coffee from the saucer. Not only did my passion for coffee begin at our kitchen table, but Grandma and her friends taught me fine table manners and the art of conversation. How fortunate I was, as a five-year-old, to be included. The coffee ritual these women shared was social, a break from the hard work they endured every day. There were no automatic washing machines, dryers or dishwashers in those days. Anna spoke English, but Swedish was the only language spoken at those coffee parties, and I soon understood every word.

Today, coffee is a giant global industry, and coffee houses have become all the rage. Coffee has come a long way since those long-ago coffee parties around our kitchen table. But this current rage isn't new. It was not only my grandmother's friends who gathered around the table for coffee and sociability. For years, men and women have been gathering for coffee in many divergent settings.

I looked forward to coffee breaks during my career as a secretary. My first coffee-break experience in 1956 was a bit intimidating. I worked for a large, international company, at one of their small office sites. Each day, the secretaries gathered with the vice presidents for their breaks. The secretaries made and served the coffee. There was no coffee talk from me for several weeks. It was different from Grandma Anna's coffee parties. Gone were the familiar faces and the Swedish chatter. But I soon became comfortable as the men shared their worldwide travel experiences to places I could only dream of visiting. Later, as a young wife and mother, I enjoyed coffee with friends and neighbors, a regular occurrence in those years.

What fun it would be to engage in some coffee talk with Grandma Anna about the latest coffee trends. She would be amazed and probably a bit confused with the variety of coffee beans available, coffee flavors, and names of some of the most popular drinks.

"Grandma Anna, I would love to introduce you to my favorite brew—a latte with espresso coffee, steamed skim milk, and a shot of vanilla, extra hot. Maybe you'd enjoy a cappuccino, a mocha, or an espresso. I haven't found a sugar cube in any of my favorite coffee houses, but you probably will not miss it."

As a writer, I enjoy getting out of the house with my laptop computer, away from daily distractions, to work at a coffee house. But I still feel the need for coffee talk. My husband and I often enjoy time together over a cup of coffee. We enjoy experimenting at home with new flavors, and a cup of coffee after dinner has become our ritual. Included in our ritual are coffee cups brought back from Sweden where we visited the places our grandparents called home.

"Even though I'm a fan of the twenty-first century coffee houses, Grandma Anna, I miss our kitchen table kaffe kalas. I enjoy many kinds of coffee, but I've never found anything that comes close to your Swedish egg coffee, and the memories of our coffee talk around the kitchen table. I no longer understand much Swedish, but you gave me the lasting gift of hospitality and a passion for coffee. For that, I give you and your friends tusen tack—a thousand thanks."

Sharon Kingan Young

Coffee Means "Ohana"

Let no man grumble when his friends fall off,
As they will do like leaves at the first breeze;
When your affairs come round, one way or
t'other, Go to the coffee house,
and take another.

Lord Byron

"**W**ould you like some coffee before we land?" the flight attendant asked as we winged our way closer to Kona on the Big Island of Hawaii.

"Please, thank you," I answered, and breathed in the delicious aroma before taking a sip.

The man in the seat next to me smiled and said, "You like coffee." It was a statement, not a question, but I answered anyway.

"I love it," and I smiled, remembering how my father also loved coffee.

He would get up early in the mornings, before the rest of us woke, brew coffee, pour his cup and sit at the kitchen table planning his day and week. Before long, my young brother would wander in and join him. Daddy would pour an inch of coffee in a cup and fill it with milk, add a spoonful of sugar, and then they would share their morning coffee together. It was a beloved ritual. Afterward, Daddy would pour another cup, carry it to the bedroom where my mother still slept, and gently wake her. No alarm has ever been so sweet for her.

"You know, I might have grown some of the beans in your coffee," my seatmate said, pulling me back to the present.

I looked at him with interest, and he continued. "Would you like to visit our coffee plantation while you're on the island?"

"We'd love to." My snoozing husband sat across the aisle so I spoke for both of us. "Where are you located?"

He pulled out his card, wrote directions on it, and said as he handed it to me, "Come in the early afternoon one day during the week, and I'll be able to give you a personal tour."

"We'll be there," I promised.

My husband shook his head and laughed when I told him about the conversation and showed him the card. "I can't take you anywhere without you striking up a friendship with some stranger." He paused and continued, "Sounds like fun. Pick a day, and we'll go."

Later in the week, sunburned and ready for an adventure, we headed for the coffee-growing hills and easily found the plantation next to the Kona Historical Society. We wandered through the quaint, old building, once a general store, which held relics and photos of days long past, showing cattle grazing on the same sloping land as the coffee farm.

Our host greeted us, pleased that we had taken him up

on his invitation, and told us that the store had once been his grandfather's, that his family had lived there and worked the land for four generations. When cattle raising became untenable, they planted coffee. He showed us trees that his grandmother had personally planted and pulled off a red bean from a cluster of berries on one of the short trees.

"This is coffee," he said, "ripe and ready for harvest. Squeeze it."

"What do you mean?"

"Just squeeze it and see what happens." He grinned.

My husband held the berry in his fingers and squeezed. Out popped a gooey substance with a small translucent bean inside.

"Taste it," we were encouraged.

"You're kidding, right?" I responded.

"No, you'll be surprised."

So we tasted the sticky paste and discovered it to be quite sweet.

"Mucilage," he told us. "It protects and feeds the coffee beans as they grow inside."

He then waved his arm up and over to indicate the thousands of coffee trees that grew on land that flowed down to the ocean. "Perfect for growing coffee, warm enough to encourage good growth, and there are showers every afternoon."

We completed the tour and saw how the beans were hand-picked, sorted, roasted, and packed for sales all over the world. We then stood under a cluster of native trees and sampled his best reserve brew.

His mother, who served as docent for the Historical Society, brought crates of fresh vegetables and fruits grown on the farm, and sat them under the tree next to the coffee. Our host's young son rode his bike nearby. We had a true sense of "ohana," which means "family" in Hawaiian. This land belonged to this family and was part of their very being. We had a new understanding and appreciation for coffee and the labor-intensive efforts it takes to bring us those cups we crave every day. Again I smiled as I remembered my father.

"Ohana." From a family in Hawaii to our small house in Georgia, we all cherish warm family memories about coffee.

Jean Stewart

10 Signs of a Coffee Lover

1. Your dream vacation is a trip to Colombia to meet Juan Valdez.

2. Your collection of coffee cups is featured on your MySpace page.

3. You chew coffee beans instead of gum.

4. All your kids are named "Joe."

5. One of the most important things you look for in a new car is the size of the cup holder.

6. You've seriously considered mortgaging your home to start a Dunkin' Donuts.

7. Your goal is to amount to a hill-of-beans.

8. When someone asks, "How are you?" you reply, "Good to the last drop."

9. You named your cats Latte and Mocha.

10. You look forward to the daily grind.

More Chicken Soup?

We would love to hear your reactions to the stories in this book. Please let us know what your favorite stories were and how they affected you.

Many of the stories and poems you have read in this book were submitted by readers like you who had read earlier Chicken Soup for the Soul books. We publish several Chicken Soup for the Soul books every year. We invite you to contribute a story to one of these future volumes.

Stories may be up to 1,200 words and must uplift or inspire. You may submit an original piece, something you have read, or your favorite quotation on your refrigerator door.

To obtain a copy of our submission guidelines and a listing of upcoming Chicken Soup books, please write, fax, or check our websites. Please send your submissions to:

Chicken Soup for the Soul
P.O. Box 30880
Santa Barbara, CA 93130
fax: 805-563-2945
website: www. chickensoup.com

Just send a copy of your stories and other pieces to the above address. We will be sure that both you and the author are credited for your submission.

For information about speaking engagements, other books, audiotapes, workshops, and training programs, please contact any of our authors directly.

Supporting Others

All over the world, millions of innocent people are caught up in intolerable situations. But they are not today's victims; they are tomorrow's heroes, who have the power to transform their own communities.

The publisher and authors of *Chicken Soup for the Chocolate Lover's Soul, Tea Lover's Soul, Coffee Lover's Soul,* and *Wine Lover's Soul* are pleased to donate five cents from the sale of each of these four books, up to $1 million per book, to Mercy Corps, an organization that exists to alleviate suffering, poverty and oppression by helping people build secure, productive and just communities.

Mercy Corps works amid disasters, conflicts, chronic poverty and instability to unleash the potential of people who can win against nearly impossible odds. Since 1979, Mercy Corps has provided $1.3 billion in assistance to people in 100 nations. Supported by headquarters offices in North America, Europe and Asia, the agency's unified global programs employ 3,400 staff worldwide and reach nearly 14.4 million people in more than 35 countries.

Mercy Corps has learned that communities recovering from war or social upheaval must be the agents of their own transformation for change to endure. It's only when communities set their own agendas, raise their own resources and implement programs themselves, that their first successes result in the renewed hope, confidence and skills to continue development.

Your purchase of this title has helped support Mercy Corps, but if you would like to do more or would like more information about the great work they do, please contact them.

Mercy Corps
3015 SW 1st Avenue
Portland, OR 97201
phone: (800) 292-3355
website: www.mercycorps.org

who Is Jack Canfield?

Jack Canfield is the cocreator and editor of the Chicken Soup for the Soul series, which *Time* magazine has called "the publishing phenomenon of the decade." The series includes more than 140 titles with over 100 million copies in print in forty-seven languages. Jack is also the coauthor of eight other bestselling books, including *The Success Principles*™: *How to Get from Where You Are to Where You Want to Be*, *Dare to Win*, *The Aladdin Factor*, *You've Got to Read This Book*, and *The Power of Focus: How to Hit Your Business, Personal and Financial Targets with Absolute Certainty*.

Jack has recently developed a telephone coaching program and an online coaching program based on his most recent book, *The Success Principles*. He also offers a seven-day Breakthrough to Success seminar every summer, which attracts 400 people from about fifteen countries around the world.

Jack is the CEO of Chicken Soup for the Soul Enterprises and the Canfield Training Group in Santa Barbara, California, and is founder of the Foundation for Self-Esteem in Culver City, California. He has conducted intensive personal and professional development seminars on the principles of success for more than a million people in twenty-nine countries around the world. Jack is a dynamic keynote speaker, and he has spoken to hundreds of thousands of others at more than 1,000 corporations, universities, professional conferences, and conventions and has been seen by millions more on national television shows such as *Oprah, Montel, The Today Show, Larry King Live, Fox and Friends, Inside Edition, Hard Copy, CNN's Talk Back Live, 20/20, Eye to Eye*, and the *NBC Nightly News* and the *CBS Evening News*. Jack was also a featured teacher in the hit movie *The Secret*.

Jack is the recipient of many awards and honors, including three honorary doctorates and a Guinness World Records Certificate for having seven books from the Chicken Soup for the Soul series appearing on the *New York Times* bestseller list on May 24, 1998.

To write to Jack or for inquiries about Jack as a speaker, his coaching programs, trainings, or seminars, use the following contact information:

Jack Canfield
The Canfield Companies
P.O. Box 30880 • Santa Barbara, CA 93130
phone: 805-563-2935 • fax: 805-563-2945
E-mail: info4jack@jackcanfield.com
www.jackcanfield.com

who Is Mark Victor Hansen?

In the area of human potential, no one is more respected than Mark Victor Hansen. For more than thirty years, Mark has focused solely on helping people from all walks of life reshape their personal vision of what's possible. His powerful messages of possibility, opportunity, and action have created powerful change in thousands of organizations and millions of individuals worldwide.

He is a sought-after keynote speaker, bestselling author, and marketing maven. Mark's credentials include a lifetime of entrepreneurial success and an extensive academic background. He is a prolific writer with many bestselling books, such as *The One Minute Millionaire, Cracking the Millionaire Code, How to Make the Rest of Your Life the Best of Your Life, The Power of Focus, The Aladdin Factor,* and *Dare to Win,* in addition to the Chicken Soup for the Soul series. Mark has made a profound influence through his library of audios, videos, and articles in the areas of big thinking, sales achievement, wealth building, publishing success, and personal and professional development.

Mark is the founder of the MEGA Seminar Series. MEGA Book Marketing University and Building Your MEGA Speaking Empire are annual conferences where Mark coaches and teaches new and aspiring authors, speakers, and experts on building lucrative publishing and speaking careers. Other MEGA events include MEGA Info-Marketing and My MEGA Life.

As a philanthropist and humanitarian, Mark works tirelessly for organizations such as Habitat for Humanity, American Red Cross, March of Dimes, Childhelp USA, and many others. He is the recipient of numerous awards that honor his entrepreneurial spirit, philanthropic heart, and business acumen. He is a lifetime member of the Horatio Alger Association of Distinguished Americans, an organization that honored Mark with the prestigious Horatio Alger Award for his extraordinary life achievements.

Mark Victor Hansen is an enthusiastic crusader of what's possible and is driven to make the world a better place.

Mark Victor Hansen & Associates, Inc.
P.O. Box 7665 • Newport Beach, CA 92658
phone: 949-764-2640 • fax: 949-722-6912
www.markvictorhansen.com

Who Is Theresa Peluso?

Theresa has always felt drawn to a page and the power of words. Books represent knowledge, expression, freedom, adventure, creativity, and escape—so it's no surprise that her life has revolved around books.

Her career began over thirty years ago in a large publisher's book-club operation. In 1981, Theresa joined Health Communications, a fledgling publisher that grew to become the country's #1 self-help publisher, home to groundbreaking *New York Times* bestsellers and the series recognized as a publishing phenomenon, *Chicken Soup for the Soul.*

Theresa is the coauthor of *Chicken Soup for the Horse Lover's Soul, Chicken Soup for the Horse Lover's Soul II, Chicken Soup for the Recovering Soul, Chicken Soup for the Recovering Soul Daily Inspirations, Chicken Soup for the Shopper's Soul, Chicken Soup for the Dieter's Soul,* and *Chicken Soup for the Wine Lover's Soul.*

She lives in south Florida with her husband, Brian, and two cats who have learned that making morning coffee takes precedence over getting their breakfast. Contact Theresa at:

Health Communications, Inc.
3201 SW 15th Street • Deerfield Beach, FL 33442
phone: 954-360-0909 • fax: 954-418-0844
e-mail: teri@coffeeloverssoul.com • website: www.hcibooks.com

contributors

The stories in this book are original pieces or taken from previously published sources, such as books, magazines, and newspapers. If you would like to contact any of the contributors for information about their writing or would like to invite them to speak in your community, look for their contact information included in their biography.

Christa Allan teaches high school English in Louisiana where she lives with her husband Ken, daughter Sarah, and their two cats. She's also mom to Michael, Erin, Shannon, John, mom-in-law to Lesley and Andrae, Grammy to Bailey, Emma, and Hannah. You can enjoy Christa's musings at www.cballan.wordpress.com as she blogs her journey to publication and beyond.

Aaron Bacall's work has appeared in most national publications, several cartoon collections, and has been used for advertising, greeting cards, wall calendars and several corporate promotional books. Three of his cartoons are featured in the permanent collection at the Harvard Business School's Baker Library. He can be reached at abacall@msn.com.

Chris Bancells has been a happily-caffeinated husband for three years now. After traveling the country with his wife, he returned to Maryland to become a writer and teacher. He has published in the *Diamondback* and *Aegis* newspapers, as well as the *Orioles* magazine. To read more, please visit www.runningbowline.com.

Marcia E. Brown is an Austin, Texas, freelance writer who is pleased to preserve family stories, especially for her grandson. Since 1993, her work has appeared regularly in magazines, newspapers and anthologies. Several of her stories have won awards.

Isabel Bearman Bucher's work ranges from research to stories of the heart. With Robert, her husband of twenty-eight years, she travels the world on home exchanges. She enjoys four children, five grandchildren, and one great-grandson. Her book, *Nonno's Monkey: An Italian-American Memoir*, is set in the 1940s and told from an oft-confused, six-year-old point of view. Visit Isabel at www.oneitaliana.com.

Gary Carroll is a former pastor in the Ohio Council of the Christian Union. He received a B.A. at Circleville Bible College, Circleville, Ohio, and graduated on Sunday, May 18, 1980, the day Mt. Saint Helens erupted.

Ruth Coe Chambers is a psychology graduate from California State University, Fresno, and the author of a novel, *The Chinaberry Album*, short stories, and articles. Her play, *Changing Places*, won first prize in the First Coast Writers' Festival Playwriting Contest in 2005, and she has recently completed a fiction manuscript and play. You can contact Ruth by e-mail at RuthCChambers@aol.com.

Harriet Cooper is a Toronto, Canada, freelance writer and humorist whose work has appeared in numerous newspapers, magazines, and anthologies. She writes on food, health, family, relationships, cats, and coffee—with milk.

Lola Di Giulio De Maci loves writing for children. Her inspiration comes from her now-grown children and the many children she has taught over the years. She is a contributor to *Chicken Soup for the Soul* books, as well as being an inspirational speaker. She writes in a sunny, sky-blue loft with a panoramic view of the San Bernardino mountains. E-mail her at LDeMaci@aol.com.

Ruth Douillette is a middle-school teacher. She writes for her town paper, and appears as a regular guest on "Around the Table," a local cable talk show. Her work has been published in the *Christian Science Monitor, flashquake*, and *Under Our Skin*, an anthology about breast cancer. Ruth is a member of the Internet Writing Workshop where she co-administers the Practice group.

Cheryl Dudley holds a Master's Degree from the University of Idaho and works in public relations. She is also a freelance writer, and has several published works, including poems, biographies, and short stories. Her first book will be published by The Lyon's Press in 2007. Cheryl continues to live in Moscow, Idaho, with her husband, Don, and their four horses.

Rhonda Eudaly lives in Arlington, Texas where she has worked in offices, banking, radio, live sound production, and education to support her writing habit and her cat, Dixon. She has a varied publication history in both fiction and non-fiction which can be found on www.RhondaEudaly.com.

Greg Faherty has had several fiction and non-fiction stories and poems published, including one in *Chicken Soup for the Teenage Soul IV*. When he and his wife are not exercising with their dogs or cooking healthy meals, he owns and operates www.a-perfect-resume.com, and also provides proofreading and editing services.

Debbie Farmer writes the nationally syndicated column "Family Daze." Her essays have appeared in several national and regional parenting magazines, as well as in several *Chicken Soup* anthologies. She lives in California and can be reached by e-mail at debbie.farmer@ yahoo.com or through her website www.familydaze.com.

Louise Foerster enjoys coffee any time, any place. The pleasures of coffee sustain her with the energy to write, walk, read, and enjoy life with her friends and family.

Cynthia Hamond has stories in numerous *Chicken Soup for the Soul* anthologies, Multnomah's *Stories for the Heart*, and major publications, including *Woman's World* magazine and King Features Syndication. She received two writing awards and was the featured author in *Anthology Today*. Two of her stories have been adapted for television. Visit her at www.Cynthiahamond.com.

Patrick Hardin is a freelance cartoonist whose work appears in a variety of periodicals and books around the world. Patrick can be reached at hardin_cartoons@comcast.net.

Jonny Hawkins has been cartooning professionally since 1986. His work has appeared in over 370 publications, such as *Reader's Digest, Forbes, Boy's Life* and *Woman's World*. His books, including *The Awesome Book of Healthy Humor* and his *Cartoon-A-Day* calendars, are available everywhere.

Jeremy R. Hope is a freelance writer and mariner who lives with his wife, two children and animals in Maryland. When he's not reading, writing, meditating, and watching things grow from his garden, he's brewing something up—either to write, sip or sing. Visit Jeremy on his website at www.wahzoonews.blogspot.com.

Dawn Howard is a full-time mom and part-time writer who writes content for websites and trade journals. This is her second contribution to the Chicken Soup for the Soul series.

Patricia Hoyt received her Master of Education degree from the University of Oregon. She taught elementary school for over twenty years and is now happily retired. Patricia spends her extra time raising exotic chickens, teaching water aerobics, gardening, and working with the youth at her church. She has previously published a story in *Chicken Soup to Inspire a Woman's Soul*.

Jennie Ivey lives in Cookeville, Tennessee. She is a newspaper columnist and author of two books, *Tennessee Tales the Textbooks Don't Tell* and *E Is for Elvis*. She has published numerous fiction and non-fiction pieces, including stories in five Chicken Soup for the Soul collections. Contact her at jivey@frontiernet.net.

Abha Iyengar is a writer, poet, cyber artist, activist, yoga enthusiast and photographer. She loves to travel and experience the new.. Her work has appeared in *Chicken Soup for the Soul Healthy Living* series, *Knit Lit Too, The Simple Touch of Fate, Arabesques Review, Scribe Spirit, Kritya, riverbabble* and *flashquake*, among others. Contact Abha by e-mail at abhaiyengar@gmail.com.

Betty King is a published author of three books, *It Takes Two Mountains to Make a Valley, But—It Was in the Valleys I Grew*, and *The Fragrance of Life*. She is a newspaper Lifestyle and Devotional columnist, and a speaker who lives with multiple sclerosis.

Mary Caffrey Knapke lives in Troy, Ohio. A graduate of Ohio University and the National University of Ireland, Galway, she has written for the Associated Press, U.S. Department of State, and a number of local and regional publications. She currently works as a freelance writer and as an English instructor at Edison Community College.

Dolores Kozielski is a certified Feng Shui practitioner in New Jersey and Pennsylvania. She is an author and an award-winning poet, published with major publishing houses including HarperCollins. Dolores is a contributor to *Chicken Soup for the Soul Healthy Living: Stress* and *Chicken Soup for the Sister's Soul 2*. She may be reached at www. FengShuiWrite.com.

Michelle Mach is a freelance writer living in Colorado. Her work has appeared in many other anthologies, including *Chicken Soup for the Shopper's Soul, Classic Christmas*, and on a coffee label for Story House Coffee. Visit her website at www.michellemach.com.

Jacqueline J. Michels is a wife, a mother, a grandmother and a humor columnist for the *Peninsula Clarion* in Soldotna, Alaska.

Rosemary Mild is coauthor, with her husband Larry, of the *Paco & Molly* mystery series: *Boston Scream Pie, Hot Grudge Sunday*, and *Locks and Cream Cheese*. She also wrote *Miriam's Gift: A Mother's Blessings— Then and Now*, a tribute to her daughter killed in the terrorist bombing of Pan Am 103 over Lockerbie, Scotland.

Eileen Mitchell is a freelance writer from Northern California. She writes the monthly "Dog's Life" column for the *San Francisco Chronicle* and is a frequent contributor to *The Bark* magazine and www.beliefnet. com. She can be reached at mitchei@sbcglobal.net.

Shana McLean Moore is the coauthor of *Femail: A Comic Collision in Cyberspace* and the author of *Caffeinated Ponderings on Life, Laughter & Lattes*. She hopes you'll stop by to savor some of her Fresh Brew by subscribing to her free newsletter at www.caffeinatedponderings.com.

Kara Newman is a New York-based food, wine, and spirits writer. She can be contacted at www.karanewman.net.

Mark Parisi's "off the mark" comic panel has been syndicated since 1987 and is distributed by United Media. Mark's humor also graces greeting cards, T-shirts, calendars, magazines, newsletters, and books. Please visit his website at www.offthemark.com. Lynn is his wife/business partner, and their daughter, Jenny, contributes with inspiration (as do three cats).

Ava Pennington is a Bible study teacher, freelance writer, public speaker, and former Human Resources Director. With an MBA from St. John's University in New York, and a Bible Studies Certificate from Moody Bible Institute in Chicago, Ava divides her time between teaching, writing, speaking, and volunteering. Contact her at rusavapen@yahoo.com.

Elizabeth H. Phillips-Hershey, Ph.D., has coauthored a middle-grade children's book, *Mind over Basketball: Coach Yourself to Handle Stress* and been published in *Appleseeds, Faces,* and *Latitudes and Attitudes*. In 1998, Elizabeth and her husband, Bob, made a passage across the Atlantic Ocean on their forty-two-foot sailboat. They sailed the Mediterranean Sea for eight years.

Kay Conner Pliszka has won numerous awards for her work with at-risk students in schools and in the community. Retired from teaching, she is now a freelance writer and speaker. Kay has stories in several *Chicken Soup for the Soul* books and was co-winner of the Chicken Soup's 10th Anniversary Short Story contest. She may be reached at kmpliszka@comcast.net.

Connie K. Pombo is an author, inspirational speaker, and founder of

Women's Mentoring Ministries in Mount Joy, Pennsylvania. She speaks to cancer groups nationwide, including the "Weekend of Hope" in Stowe, Vermont where she first found her passion for writing. She can be reached at www.conniepombo.com and www.womensmentoringministries.com.

Kay Presto is an award-winning book author, photographer and former talk show host. She is an international professional speaker and has been a reporter on CNN Television and Mutual Radio. Honors for her writing include the 2005 Woman of Achievement Award from the National Association of Female Executives (NAFE) in New York. She also honors seniors at www.shirts4seniors.com. Kay can be reached at prestoprod6@verizon.net.

Carol McAdoo Rehme directs a nonprofit agency, Vintage Voices, Inc. She is a prolific writer, editor and coauthor of numerous gift books. Her latest project, *Chicken Soup for the Empty Nester's Soul*, will be released in 2008. Contact her at carol@rehme.com.

Kayleen J. Reusser has published more than 2,000 articles in newspapers, books, and magazines, including *Today's Christian Woman*, *Indianapolis Monthly*, and *Ft. Wayne News-Sentinel*. This is Kayleen's third story published in the *Chicken Soup for the Soul* series. She can be reached at Kjreusser@adamswells.com or at www.KayleenR.com.

Victoria Roder is the Director at Zion Lutheran Day Care, and enjoys writing in her free time. She has published a script with *One Way Street*, her work has appeared in *Farm Life Magazine*, and she has just finished her first novel. Victoria lives in the country with her family and pets.

Sallie A. Rodman is an award-winning writer whose stories have appeared in various *Chicken Soup* anthologies and magazines. She and her husband live in Southern California where they enjoy their favorite coffee at the local Starbucks; he—extra strong regular, she—carmelita macchiato. E-mail her at sa.rodman@verizon.net.

Donald Rogers is a former Seattle Fire Captain who now works for the Mariners during baseball season. Coffee helped carry him through a twenty-five-year career and has remained a dependable morning companion for the ten years of house remodeling, elder care-giving and alpine skiing since his retirement.

Maureen Rogers is a transplanted Canadian living in the Seattle area, known by many as the coffee capital of the world. She has been published in newspapers, anthologies and online. Her writing projects include fiction, poetry, and essays, all generated by at least two morning cups of coffee.

Debbie Roppolo is a freelance writer residing in the Texas hill country with her husband and two children. Her writing has appeared in anthology collections such as *Chicken Soup for the Dog Lover's Soul*, and in online and print publications.

Julie B. Sevig is a writer and associate editor of *The Lutheran* magazine in Chicago, Illinois. As a mother of three children under age four, her favorite song is "The Coffee Song" by Ralph's World: "M-o-m-m-y needs c-o-f-f-e-e." Her family table prayer book, *Peanut Butter and Jelly Prayers*, is available from Morehouse Publishing.

Barbara Smith is a freelance writer/editor and medical ethicist; Emerita Professor of Literature and Writing and Former Chair of the Division of the Humanities, Alderson-Broaddus College, Philippi, West Virginia. More importantly, and in addition to keeping at least six coffee companies in business, she is a sports nut.

Joyce Stark lives in Northeast Scotland and has recently retired from local government. She has just completed her first book about her travels in the USA and is working on her second book aiming to teach another language to very young children. You can reach her at joric.stark@virgin.net.

Jean Stewart is a writer residing in Mission Viejo, California, with her husband of forty-six years and is the mother of twin daughters. Her family, parenting, and travel stories can be found in other *Chicken Soup for the Soul* books, as well as newspapers and magazines.

Theresa Theiler, along with her husband, three dogs and a cat, lives near her family. She is the author of *Soul Stories; Personal Transformational Myths*, as well as other stories and articles.

Cristy L. Trandahl is a freelance writer and mother of six. She contributes to many nationally distributed anthologies and speaks on parenting issues. For more information, visit Cristy's website at www.cristytrandahl.com.

Ellen Hunter Ulken has written *Beautiful Dreamer, The Life of Stephen Collins Foster*, and a short biography of *Bernard de Marigny de Mandeville, Statesman, Gambler, Founder of the City of Mandeville*, available through the St. Tammany Parish Historical Society in Louisiana. Ellen now lives in Peachtree City, Georgia and writes essays for publication.

Samantha Ducloux Waltz is a freelance writer in Portland, Oregon. Her personal essays are her favorite way to sort out her always-interesting, often-chaotic world, and can be seen in a number of current anthologies and *The Christian Science Monitor*.

Debra Weaver is a writer and educator with experience across a wide range of audiences. She has taught students from preschool to high school and trained adults in workplace skills. Her latest project is launching a coaching program for aspiring writers.

Cheryl Elaine Williams is a retired freelance writer residing in western Pennsylvania. She enjoys family activities, writers' functions, gardening and raising pet parakeets.

Shannon Woodward writes and edits from Marysville, Washington, where she lives with her husband (a Calvary Chapel pastor) and their two children. She is a columnist for *Christian Women Online*, a contributor to several anthologies and the author of three nonfiction books. Visit Shannon at www.shannonwoodward.com or www.windscraps.blogspot.com.

Mary K. Young is retired from a career in public service, and worked in a part-time capacity for many years for a local daily newspaper, *The Punxsutawney Spirit*, writing news stories, features, and a column entitled "My Family and Me." Mary has three sons, five grandchildren, and presently shares her home with two very spoiled cats.

Sharon Kingan Young resides in west Des Moines, Iowa. Her work has been published in *A Cup of Comfort for Weddings: Something Old, Something New*, and in magazines including *The Iowan, ByLine, Collectors News*, and *GRIT*.